Bob Flowerdew's
Autoby**Bob**raphy volume V

Vendange heureuse, Vin dangereux

Grape picking in Beaujolais -un Raisin d'être

Vendange heureuse, Vin dangereux
Grape picking in Beaujolais -un Raisin d'être,

"Avez-vous besoin d'un autre vendangeur?" she carefully enunciated while she wrote these words out in block capitals on the back of a small piece of card.
"This says; have you need of another grape-harvester? It's all you need to say."
I read it back to her, the look on her face was dubious.
"Ah Bob, perhaps best you say nothing, just show them this card, your French pronunciation is, it's, it's painful."
 "Please, just stand here in the market place right in front of the Mairie, our French town hall. In small towns in every fruit area farmers come to this same spot looking for pickers, it's their traditional hiring method. Look, over there, those people, they'll be doing the same, why don't you join them, and Bob, remember, all you have to do is just the same as everyone else does."
With my thanks I shut her car door and she drove off. I stood there in the market place of a small rural town in the middle of France. The dawn was reddening the near cloudless sky above mist laden rounded green hills looming in ranks all round.

The market was already busy, some selling, several still setting up their stalls. Folk were going through the steaming Boulangerie (Bakers) doors emerging with loaves of bread, oddly though many carried not the usual ubiquitous long stick like baguettes I knew so well but large round loaves wrapped in paper, sometimes stacks of several.
Some more arrivals getting off a bus walked past the stalls straight into the noisy smoky depths of an old regime café with etched windows and flaking paint. A couple of the guys came back out and stood outside smoking, I could tell by the acrid smell, Camel cigarettes. From that and their appearance, German or Dutch I reckoned; tanned with worn rucksacks they looked as if they'd already been working the fields all summer.
Seemed a good place to start so I wandered over with
 "Hi I'm Bob, do you speak English?"
One stubbed his cigarette butt on his heel, introduced himself and his friend. They were Dutch, had started picking fruit down by the Mediterranean coast earlier in the year, working their way through the fruit harvests, earning and learning as they went, they were intending running a fruit farm of their own one day.
Having finished picking peaches and other fruits

further south they were now looking for work here, though thought it was almost over.

I told them how returning from hitch-hiking to Morocco I'd run out of cash so needed to find at least enough to pay for the Dover night-ferry home. Picking grapes had seemed an appealing solution.

"I've been warned you work damn hard but in return got accommodation, your food and drink, as well as paid."

(This had sounded brilliant as you say goodbye to regular, well to almost any, meals when you hitch-hike.)

"I grew up on a farm and picked fruits and vegetables for summer jobs, though of course we never picked grapes in England!"

They laughed, and pointed out they would be finishing their grape picking season with the northern French and German white wines -so why do we not grow grapes in England?

I laughed at the thought, then continued optimistically

"Anyway I'm sure I'll find this easy and make some cash."

They laughed again. It seemed that although you were indeed given bed & board few pickers ever made it home with much cash from picking grapes. The problem was you became used to eating and drinking very heavily. For while you picked you got unlimited wine, not just with meals but all the day through. Who could resist, the wine flowed freely, so most drank several bottles a day apiece, easily. However once the Vendange was over your habit would carry on at the same rate, and before many days were up you'd drunk your cash away.

"I'd not be so foolish" I foolishly said. I was of course wrong.

While we were chatting another couple came over, they too were looking for work. All agreed it was sensible to wait in the market place for hiring, though it was a bit of a chance as to what sort of work you might get it was the only way. One guy pointed out it was the same from the other side, after all the farmer does not know who he will get and whether they will be any use or even stay till the end.

I asked why one farmer could not simply pass pickers on to another, then they'd both know what to expect and if it was likely to be okay either way.

The problem seemed typically rural, the only other farmers most farmers knew were local farmers, so when you had done at one farm all the others nearby would be finishing as well. Thus you had to follow the harvest as it moved north, by some distance, to another more northerly market place.

So Chantal had been right, this was their way, you simply stood in front of a Mairie during harvest time and farmers needing pickers would come.
The others chatted on about the risks and rewards, and awful stories, you never knew what you might end up with. After all some places were simply not well run, and could even be seriously dangerous. Not so much from criminals but simple from drunken brawls.
Every year several Vendangeurs ended up in the local hospital. However despite that grim possibility there were also the bad farmers with mean facilities and meaner food.
The Dutch guys told of their last farm where their meals had been bread soup with bread and wine and not much else. Still, they noted even at that worst they had had unlimited wine, after all that cost the producers nothing, and you could always fill yourself with as many grapes as you could eat.
We saw more folk arriving and standing the other side of the Mairie steps so we shuffled over to chat with them.
The sun was beginning to shine over the roofs around us when a mud besplattered grey Peugot pickup rattled into view, slowed down and stopped with a jerk by our little group. The driver wound down his window, started saying

stuff rapidly in French to which the others responded. By this time I had my piece of card out ready when the others grabbed me, a quick shove and about a half dozen of us were in the back of the pickup and on our way.

Some scarily unnerving, uncomfortable, undoubtedly unlawful driving later we arrived in a sea of grapevines flowing picturesquely over misty mountainous hillside. Neat rows of wires, stakes and vines in geometric patterns. In the blue green distance it resembled folds of cloth of rough tweed. In the rows nearest where our pickup lurched to a halt a line of folk were bent over picking grapes part way up the hillside. We jumped out. Leaving our bags in a pile by the side of the road a few minutes later we were armed with a 'sooh' (bucket) and a 'sir-pet' a strange knife with a curled end, and we started picking grapes alongside the rest of the 'ee-kip' (team).

The strange knife, 'sir-pet' as I heard it, was made from a rigid steel rod, one end bent into a loop held round your little finger. The rod nestled across the base of your other curled fingers then projected a little beyond your thumb where it was flattened into a small curved sickle the size of a walnut. The only sharp edge was inside the curve which would neatly part the stalks holding bunches without cutting anything else. This simple, safe-knife would do little accidental damage to the vines or bunches, and perhaps not incidentally was very economic to make. It was also not a very handy weapon to use for deliberate harm to other pickers in those not uncommon drunken disputes.

I was paired with one of the older pickers who showed me how to pick, which to pick and what to reject- all in perfect rapid French so I understood not a word, but it was all fairly obvious, or at least I thought so.

After all it was fruit picking and I'd done plenty of that so no problem. Though coming from a flat county I was unused to working on a slope. On a slope you worked up hill which reduced the bending a tad, lifting each bunch away with one hand as you snicked through the stalk with the sir-pet held in the other and transferred it to your bucket.

Grapevines are grown many ways, in this system the old woody vines were running along wires held below knee height with another set of wires about shoulder high. The old vines sprouted yard / metre long shoots which had been spaced out and tied up to the top wires with the bunches of grapes hanging in array from these. Very neat, you could see each bunch sprung from a new shoot about five leaves or so from where this started from the old vine in spring.

Much like I'd seen vines growing on walls in some greenhouses back in England.
Depending on the variety often Pinot or Gamay, the weather so far and now, the soil, the pruning, even the age of the vines, caused the size of the bunches to vary. Sometimes these were large, bloated, with tender skins bursting as you held them. These were also likely to have mouldy parts, which needed cutting out discarding the rotten berries on the ground so only clean grapes went in your bucket. Other times the bunches could be compact of small tight berries and strong skins, a joy to pick by comparison. Small bunches were also easier to hold while you picked another, or several, at one pass. When you thought you'd picked clean you'd give the vines a shake to show if any bunches were hiding, and there were often a few small ones. All the time you moved up hill lifting up and moving along your bucket putting each or bunch or bunch of bunches into the bucket carefully. Too many rammed in would crush the grapes letting the juice and air mix so when a bucket was full a fellow I heard pronounced as 'jhzolloo' would be summoned to appear. He carried an enormous oval half barrel into which three or more pickers would empty their buckets. The picker from the row he was in, and those from rows on either side would pass their buckets

through from the other side of their wires or tip them in from over the top. He would then carry all these bucket-fulls of grapes in his half barrel downhill to even larger containers, huge wooden barrel like trugs, standing at the bottom of the rows.

The pace, as with any manual task not on piece rate, naturally slackens, while the bosses always want the crop picked more rapidly. More so with grapes, not just for economy but as speedy collection and processing is necessary to make good wine (as the grapes are easily burst they start to bleed and the juice then gets exposed to the air and can go 'vinegary').

So the old hands went at a fair rate and we novices were 'encouraged' to keep up, laggards were 'aided' by a flying helper. Their role was to keep all the pickers working at the same level across the rows so as to minimise the work of the 'jhzolloo' staggering up and down.

All to get those grapes as fast as possible to the fermentation vats before they degraded.

The crazy drive we had experienced in the Peugot on the way over was as nothing compared to racing manoeuvres we saw as veteran scarred pickups speeded overloaded stacks of overflowing containers down the hill to the 'cave' for processing.

Now I enjoy physical exertion, always have so there was little problem with the work, apart from the sustained effort, but that was par for the course anyway. As I had picked fruit and vegetables many times before I understood the need for getting a rhythm, of moving effectively, efficiently, without wasting effort. Your eyes and hands start to work almost independently, but you have to supervise, and this means moving deliberately.

Field work is a day long work-out, you need develop skill as well as stamina if you are to keep going at a pace. You do not shuffle about but take a comfortable stance where you can pick around the vine front and both sides, then move to another position to clear the remainder. Each of your deliveries ferrying several rather than one bunch each time to the bucket. The bucket resting on the ground and only being picked up and moved a minimal number of times. Then once the vine is picked over, checked with a shake, you stretch and move up to the next vine.

Now I'm competitive, and usually working on piece rate back home had made me fast, thus I soon became an obviously proficient picker. ie not only were all the grapes in my bucket clean, I did not miss many on the vines, and I was usually well up ahead not lagging.

By comparison with what I had done in the past this work seemed much preferable. To any experienced fruit picker grapes are a breeze, they have no vicious thorns like gooseberries or blackberries, nor few but treacherously sharp bristles like raspberries, nor wasps like apples and plums. The bending was severe but nowhere near as far over as for strawberries, or for spuds, or sugar beet, both of which were also muddy and cold. Hey, picking grapes was really not so bad, and most days the weather was nice and warm, I hate cold and love working in the warm. Indeed I found even the hottest days no problem when most of the others were finding the heat too much.

And I liked eating grapes, in quantity, fruits I'd never seen close up or tried more than a handful of times before. Turned out these grown for wine were really sweet, just smaller berried than the few commercial dessert type grapes I had eaten in the past. Best of all when picking was every so often you came across a vine of another variety of grapes that were 'not to be collected', these were for pollination, or a mistake, I was never quite sure. These were excellent eating though, the cropping vines here had dark red to black smallish grapes but these pollinator grapes were huge sweet white berries and so delicious.

The morning passed with the sun warming all those bunches exposed till they became almost hot to the hand while bunches inside the shade of the leaves stayed cold often still coated in dew. Plop, plop, plop went the bunches into the buckets, vine after vine, row upon row. In early afternoon we were halted and led to some trestle tables set out on the wide roadside verge. A cauldron of thick soup, piles of bread, cheese, sausage, and bowls of fruit. Flasks of coffee and flagons of wine. Simple food but when you've been working in the fresh air it always tastes so good, really satisfying.

Now although we had been expected to work hard for hours the lunch break was not rushed, indeed it was to my mind a tad too long. But then traditionally lunch in France always has been. Their quip was you needed a long lunch to both eat well and satisfy your lover -which freed you up for later that day with your partner, after a good dinner of course.

We sat around on our buckets eating while folk were chatting in what seemed at least a half dozen languages. The Vendange brought pickers from all over Europe. Fortunately many spoke some English, sometimes very well, and some could speak several languages so were translating between others. Most certainly had better than my language skills. (Someone once

quipped if you speak many languages you were a polyglot, if you spoke two then you're bi-lingual, and if you speak only one you're English.)
How little French I spoke- *a digression*, I had learnt a little French at school despite extra lessons with the French student (with whom of course I became besotted) and learning a tad more on visits with student friends. They'd inherited an apartment in the very centre of Paris, Rue du Louvre, very near The Louvre, it was behind big old doors with a concierge, ancient, and then up a hundred and more steps, wonderful place to stay. Spent many college holidays there partying, having student fun, drinking too much and particularly exploring my interest in varieties of French cheese, in exchange bringing over British cheeses for comparison. Now Paris was smaller than London, almost all the places of interest were concentrated in the old city with many in walking distance. And my friends had a Mini-Cooper, a small car designed for nipping through awful traffic, then compact to somehow find a parking place –which often required amazingly complicated slow speed manoeuvres to squeeze into some tiny space. I'd got to know central Paris, sort of, when a friend who was working as an Official Guide got ill and I was asked to stand in for them. Now as I said my French was worse

than rubbish, but no problem, apparently. I was to accompany a bus of British kids, the driver would know where to go etcetera all I had to do was answer questions –in English. Well I'd give it a go so I took badge and papers and set off to join my bus. I got on board and was passed a microphone by a teacher so I could talk about the historical sights we were driving past. I had a map with me thus was doing a fair job as the bus crawled along giving me time to read ahead. Admittedly my introduction to Paris did include a disproportionate number of cheese varieties which somehow got into my chatter, after all, I had little else 'French' to talk about, well not to children. We disgorged, wandered around then visited Notre Dame, which was a doddle, our batch of teachers and kids just joined the queue of others and I waffled my way in, round and out again. Then we went to the Palais de Justice, which was a great pile of similar architecture, however despite having just read the guide on the map I was well caught out. We queued to get into St Chapelle, a church inside the palace. This was built in 1248 and from outside looked like another pile of stone pillars and buttresses. We trooped in with me wittering on about having visited almost every day for months, when we emerged inside the most amazing jewelled light display I'd ever seen. I gasped "oh my god", and realising I was giving the game away frantically crossed myself and added "forgive a poor sinner, Amen."

I had reason to be stunned, it was a bright sunny day and this chapel was the finest and unique early example of tall perpendicular walls not surrounding but radiating outwards so you only saw their inner ends. With glorious technicolour stained glass filling all the large spaces up and between. You appeared to be in an enormous jewelled lantern. Fortunately it was so impressive they forgot about my odd behaviour and poor commentary, though there were a few difficult questions later while they had their packed lunches. Well we continued our tour in the afternoon but by then the teachers were becoming more and more concerned with controlling their kids who were becoming fractious than by my lack lustre performance. On my return to my friends and handing over the badge and papers they asked how it had gone. I reckoned okay. At that point one of them burst out laughing, I'd been an Official Guide, a man who understood less French than his mother's poodle! He then bet I'd talked a lot about cheese, how did he guess?

Speaking French was not essential but at least attempting to speak French was, it gained the traveller in France respect for their effort. Also, with some trips under my belt I had picked up that while resorting to *speaking* English was okay however *being* English was not generally the best option. There were many folk in France (and Spain) who were not friendly to the British for quite justifiable historical reasons. Thus when I also observed the warm welcomes with which my United Kingdom compatriots were greeted I started wishing to be Scots or Irish rather than English. Not wanting to deceive just for a quiet life as it obviously antagonised far fewer. Indeed it was such a profound difference I had soon adopted a faux Scots accent, which fitted with my red tinged blonde hair and sun bronzed skin.

That is it fitted well enough until that lunch that first day picking grapes when a genuine Scot called me out grossly offended with my awful stereotypical portrayal. Though when I explained it was to avoid being spotted by the French or Spanish as their English foe he seemed so amused he immediately forgave me. Though he then reckoned I really could not have Scottish blood as that was such an English deception.

We returned to the picking, full of food, sleepy with wine and really wanting to doze. A long long afternoon followed. So beautiful though, the rolling hills covered in their sombre autumn patchwork splattered here and there with little splatters of spotted colour where other folk were picking. The peaceful rural quiet interrupted by overheating engines and gearboxes protesting with horns blaring as another unstable overloaded pickup would fly past, or whine more slowly but just as frenetically on the return back up.

So slowly the sun finally approached the tops of the surrounding hills, and long shadows stretched over the fields, phew it was coming to an end. Someone called Fin, others called back Vin.

Generally rejoicing, we milled around, and drank yet more wine. Then, consternation, it seemed we had only been hired for the one day, to finish off this farms' vines. We extra workers were not needed tomorrow, nor were there beds as such though we could sleep in one of the barns. Of course being France they naturally needed to provide a meal and wine for us, which was the soup and other leftovers from earlier. The farmer then offered to drop us in the nearest town at daybreak when we could tout for work at the Mairie.

An early morning rise, coffee and wine offered and taken, and we were off in his grey pickup at breakneck speed. Myself and other pickers were dropped in the town square and we went to sit on the town hall steps. It was quiet, hour after hour passed and no farmers were coming. We went to a café nearby where we could watch from, and of course drink some wine. I listened occasionally while they chatted to the locals understanding the odd bit here and there. Understood more when another couple, from Belgium, joined us (okay they translated the gist for me). Seemed there was no point being here, all the local farmers had finished Vendange so no more pickers would be needed, we had to move further North.

Fortunately the new couple had a VW campervan, and would let me ride with them as the folk I'd been with decided to take a taxi to the next area, an expense I'd not wanted to incur with only one days pay so far. We set off, myself in the back crammed in amongst an amazing amount of gear as well as my own over-loaded backpack. Apart from being a tad cramped I enjoyed the journey as we slowly drove northwards, winding roads up and down hills and valleys. Glorious scenery, beautiful, rustic, ancient, unspoilt, only problem was, as we could see, the grapes had nearly all been picked. The couple stopped whenever we saw anyone who might be or know of a farmer needing pickers, we, well they, asked each one we came to. Go further north they all said. We drove on, seemed to take all day though looking at a map it was not so far. We stopped in a small town to get some food and wine, and found out there were farmers still picking but it was after-noon so we should come back to the Mairie in the morning... So we went to a café to have a glass of wine and before we noticed it was getting dark, and wet, showers kept coming and going. We drove out of the town looking for somewhere to stop. Finding a bit of rough land between fields of grapes we parked up. They had a tent but would sleep in the comfort of the campervan as it was raining, I could have their tent, though I would have to put it up. Luckily I had a small (though still too damn heavy) tent in my back-pack which I could set up blindfolded. When the rain abated I rushed to get it up in record time and got inside. With a cheery wave I closed up, only to open up again very soon after being illuminated by car headlights with French shouting and similar shouting back again from the campervan with me twixt the two. Someone then fell over maybe deliberately kicked my lines so my wee tent collapsed around me. Scrambling out there's this chap, with a grey Peugot pickup, shouting amongst other things "papiers, papiers." Now as I said my French was limited but I could understand he was wanting to see our papers, I could also see he was no policeman and from his appearance and dress much more likely a local farmer. I amazed myself as in almost understandable French I said "Papiers, papiers, vous demandez notre papiers, ou est votre papiers?" Then went on in English "I come here to pick grapes, it rains and I'm trying to sleep in my tent so I can look for work tomorrow. You're no policeman, what's your problem? He replied, in surprisingly good English that he thought we were thieves preparing to rob his nearby farm. Which I found really funny, hysterically so and started pointing to my pile of wet tent. "`My god your thieves are different, in England they would be embarrassed to set up a wee tent like this before robbing you, they always put up huge marquees with flashing lights." I don't know whether he understood my sarcasm or whether he just twigged it was indeed unlikely we were planning a raid by first setting up a tent. The campervan on it's own could have aroused genuine doubts, but with a tent... Which collapsed tent was now wet and unwelcomingly becoming wetter and wetter in the rain with the weight of the wet fly sheet laying on the inner. He apologised and said we could move into his farmyard where they could park and I could sleep in a barn. Which again turned out not so bad with plenty of hay, I was ok, wet and snuggling in hay in a barn, just like going back to childhood.

In the morning he woke us early with a jug of coffee and reported he'd called around and found a nearby farmer who could use us though again for just one day. Only another one day, but then this farmer would try and arrange us more work with his brother afterwards, several of his pickers were going there already apparently. Brilliant, and it was just down the road, he drove ahead and we soon arrived, very near and above the very fields we'd been parked next to. Indeed though much much further up the hillside.

It was steep, very steep, mind bogglingly steep as the narrow fields clung to the contours. There were tracks running across most of the faces of the incline, backwards and forwards many times with scary hairpin turns at each end. In between each run of tracks were long thin fields (field infers too large a place, often these were small though still substantial plots). These stretched up the hillsides to the point where scrub took over, everywhere they were planted with grapevines clinging to stakes stuck like prickles on the slopes. Each vine had its own stake it was tied to with no wires to get in the way. The shoots had sprung from a stump of old vine, ballooned out to then be gathered in and tied together again at shoulder height or so. Sort of like a half open umbrella on top of another upside down one. The grapes hung part way, four or five leaves up, and partly inside. Depending on the size of the bunches and the density of foliage more bunches were hidden than on wires.

But the problem was the steepness, no wonder they left these vines till last, they were going to be hard to pick. Now I understand how as it was high up thus colder so these were also late to ripen. Conveniently the angling towards the sun compensated with better exposure and plenty of airflow which kept the moulds at bay so these were mostly lovely clean grapes.

Though it was to prove as hard work as predicted, the land rose so steeply you had to grasp onto a vine to keep your balance whilst picking bunches, alternately with both hands, simultaneously stopping your bucket tumbling away by holding this between your knees and the vine you're picking. Best not to consider what would happen if you fell, though it would never be all the way to the valley bottom as you'd be sure to come to a quick stop on the next cross track down, small comfort.

For laying down on the track would be likely as dangerous as the fall itself for up and down this mountainous track were spluttering and whining those damn Peugot pickups, overladen with grapes, racing as if their life did not matter. Nor your life, if you had fallen onto the track I doubt they'd have stopped, not out of ruthlessness but inability, so overloaded and so fast were they hurtling down they just could not have come to a halt.

So of course in typical French fashion when "a soupe" a second breakfast in the field was called they arranged our picnic along a lower section of track where it widened just enough to allow us to flinch against the near cliff face behind us or be winged by the pickups hurtling past. I was so hungry the bread and soup was wonderful, I even ventured to try morsels of the sausages as these looked so appetising, and were, though full of chunks of fat, something I'd not seen often in British cuisine. I seldom ate much meat and noticed it is fat not meat that carries the flavour, bread and sausage may have been simple fare, but these were simply excellent. I also tried another French breakfast staple, chocolate-with-bread, which was better than I expected and packed enough calories to compete with our British bacon butty though not the gamut of savoury flavour of course. (Smoked bacon was one of the few meats I found difficult to give up, as with coffee, half the thrill is in the smell and aroma anticipating the prospect of the taste to come.)

But, second breakfast was not lunch, before we had half recovered we were off again up the slopes. That morning was tiring work, and dirtier with scrambling up the hill, often dragging yourself up by the vines or even weeds. Soon learned never hold onto the stakes the vines were tied to as these just snapped off. The vines themselves were like cables though and firmly anchored, and though the grapes were often soil splashed which was not good they were free from rot and mould and nicely ripe so at least simple to pick.

As we worked away the bits of field became even steeper, each run more vertiginous than the last, I could not see how we could pick those that would be coming after lunch any way other than with a helicopter. The sun beat down hotter across the slopes and as midday passed it became incredibly more beautiful, the blue sky above green and russet hills, the patchwork of fields below us. Then hearing the bell from a church down in the valley sounding the hours. It was surprisingly quiet up here otherwise with the traffic noise seemingly filtered and distant far below. It was then I twigged what was so different. Sure these were fields of grapes not sugar beet or wheat but otherwise this was countryside much like I'd known during my childhood on our farm. There were fields, ditches, hedges, meadows, woody bits, here and there some poultry, not much livestock though quite a few places had rabbit hutches outside. (We used to keep those, good tucker, better than wild as not so gamey.) The difference was so few wild birds, there were just very few, which was odd considering the percentage of 'wild wood' and scrub, and the sheer amount of grapes on offer stretching over distant hills as far as you could see.

As the sun became fiercely overhead we stopped for lunch, another picnic on the track edge, much the same as the breakfast but more so, with more baskets of bread, flagons of wine, jugs of coffee, soup and pieces of quiches, pizza, vegetable flans, cold cuts, cheese and fruit etcetera. However the best improvement was those Peugot pickups also stopped hurtling past during lunch, indeed everything stopped, other than the drinking and chattering.

We even had time for a quick snooze in the shade, then it was back to work. And the steepest slopes were now about to be tackled. Some of the pickers were fixing ropes to spikes they were hammering in at the tops of rows. Then, yes, they were lowering themselves down the slope between the rows with the ropes stopping them tumbling. With their rope held fast round their waists they were then picking the grapes into their buckets, which when full they lowered on other ropes to folk collecting and emptying below. Umm, could see they might have done this before. I gratefully stuck to my lot picking the slightly less mountainous rows - which were scary enough.

The sun was setting, well hiding behind the hills and without it the air felt chill. We'd finished anyway, and when the last barrels of grapes had been whisked off the trusty Peugots returned to collect us. Then in a jubilant mood they drove us down to the farm at even more than their usual insane rate with us all digging our fingernails into the metalwork in abject fear. Boy did I need that drink when we staggered out back by the cave in the farmyard.

The couple with the campervan I'd arrived with had suddenly decided they were driving back up to Belgium and did not want to move on to the next farm. However as I'd had explained to me several pickers were going to this farmer's brother's farm and I could go along with those. No problem, I had my back pack, and sat, tired as heck but happy, sun burnt and dirty, with a series of glasses of wine. I was quite sleepy when another Peugot suddenly appeared and we were off into the looming night, all crammed in the back of yet another indistinguishable grey dusty Peugot pickup, on yet another, even scarier, roller coaster ride.

The dark winding roads went on and on. Admittedly we were tired, and more than a little drunk for we'd all been drinking to assuage our hunger. Large flagons of wine were to hand so we passed them round, and round again. It seemed an unduly long journey until we arrived at our destination by which time we were barely able to stand as we stumbled out.

A huge old barn loamed in front of us, indeed a medieval barn, a massive door and inside all gloomy with a single electric light bulb hanging on a thin wire from a high beam incongruously large enough to support a horse. A dozen or so old army style beds, some with sleeping bodies, were at one end, and thank goodness, a table with, yes, bread soup and bread. My god that tasted good, and the second, and third bowl. Then I immediately fell onto an empty bed, and was asleep in seconds.

Moments later we were being woken by someone hammering a metal pail, more soup, bread and coffee, and jars with loose Gaulloise cigarettes for those who smoked, breakfast had arrived along with our new boss.

It was hard to imagine this man had not been the original model for the French postcard peasant farmer. A swollen red nose, inebriated, Gaulloise stub on lip, beret wearing, shabby blue overalls, worn wellies, with a guilty hangdog look. He seemed as if sent from central casting. Then it became more surreal, like seeing the set of an old black and white film, for stood outside the barn in the grey misty light before dawn was his aged wooden cart with even older shaggy horse, no longer common even in rural France, a sight lingering from the previous century.

We were greeted (hands just have to be shaken all round) and each given a glass of wine to drink, with barely time to wash and eat our soup with haste we scurried to follow the cart to the fields. The sun was coming up and the Vendange must proceed with all speed.

Here the ground was flatter, less hilly, the vines were bushes tied to stakes again, also in rows but much longer rows, each vine a metre or so apart, a metre or so high, repeatedly in every direction. The absence of wires getting in the way was again as convenient as it had been on the hill but as this was flatter ground so you had to bend the more.

Our picking stopped after a couple of hours and we were given a second breakfast of more soup, more coffee, more wine. Many were mixing soup and wine, something I thought was odd for breakfast. I asked if this was usual and told "they mix in your stomach anyway". It was assumed you would drink wine at every opportunity and so plenty was provided in great quantity. I was there to earn a living, a few pickers it seemed were there more as a drinking holiday. And to be fair it seemed many locals drank as much as most of them anyway. Well at least some did, for on odd days and over weekends friends, family and children would also all be pressed to join the Vendange.

Thus water or thin fruit squash was usually available for the 'family' but most pickers much preferred a tumbler of wine whenever thirsty. As long as you still worked the farmers did not care how happy you got, and on this farm this so traditional farmer loved to be happy too. For if you paused, stood up and called 'unn-tasz' he came to you with a flagon, and two dirty tumblers, one for each of you. You had to down your drink as quick as he for he would down his then be off to the next. Over one day I counted him drink forty or more glasses of wine, with presumably even more swigged unseen. No wonder he had a throbbing red nose.

His job was made easier by his horse, a shaggy old mare, and as I discovered a biter. She had a hard job. Her heavy cart had to be moved short distances over very rough terrain, getting even heavier with each move. Then burdened to tumbling point it needed pulling back to the 'cave' and cellars. While she stood waiting time upon time she nibbled at whatever was in reach, including your backside if you were unwise enough to pick whilst she was near. She knew her job so well he seldom ever had to tell her when to pull forward. She knew, would just move to the next pick up spot and wait while the right number of trugs were loaded, then move again on to the next.

As I noted the picking here was surprisingly even harder work as there was no slope so you had to bend down the more, but at least there weren't those damn wires getting in the way like my first place. You could reach around the top of each clump picking from either side, though there always remaining bunches hidden inside and so harder to spot than on wires. These vines were so much bigger and bushier, and denser, than either those on wires or those on the hill. And they carried a lot of bunches. I learned to rock the bush so I could sense their position from their shaking and pick those bunches felt but unseen. Something you might not do so readily using an ordinary sharp knife, now the curled blade of the sir-pet made even more sense!

Some of the vines we went to pick that day were in a corner field on the edge of the 'wilder' land beyond. These were all old, gnarled and not very vigorous, indeed looked pretty miserable, on these the grapes were all oddly small, in perfect miniature bunches. I ate quite a few, the flavour and sweetness were so intense, and the tiny berries were often seedless, yummy like nougat. I was being shouted at, I thought it was for stopping to eat but in fact I was being told off for eating those grapes (as I learned later when others translated what had happened). Seems these were The finest most Venerable vines on The most Valuable Terroire, and those *tiny grapes* were the *essential essence* for the whole *estates'* wine, and I had just pigged an appreciable quantity. Ooops C'est la vie, or was it C'est le vin.

It was while being informed as to which I was and wasn't supposed to eat I started to understand a bit more about the language around grapes. It was not as it sounded to an English speaker. Grappes were the bunches of berries called raisins. You can see how this happened, the first fruits to get to Blighty will have been dried ones, which were called 'Raisin' (actually Raisin sec/dried). Later as transport got faster a fresh bunch could make it to Blighty, which to a Brit were manifestly not 'Raisins' those dried up rat dropping like chewy things. So the fresh fruit bunches were described in French = Grappe and so we have been misnaming the fresh berries since. Raisins have remained the name for the dried fruits in English. This complicated by there being a variety of small seedless berry from Corinth particularly good for drying which became called Currants. Along with Sultanas (Sultan's concubines) for dried whitish yellow grapes, and Muscat raisins with a gorgeous spiciness.

That night in the barn the inevitable soup was accompanied by numerous platters of bread, cheese, several sorts of sausage and ham, fruits, and generously though oddly to me, those tumblers of Gaulloises cigarettes. And of course more wine. Life was good, and sleep was deep, and short.

Too soon it was morning, another day, more soup, more wine, more picking, fall in bed. Too soon it was morning, another day, more soup, more wine, more picking, fall in bed. Too soon it was morning, another day, more soup, more wine...

The back-ache, sore knees, calloused and scratched hands and arms, heck it was just like back home on the farm again. But with a warm sun, enough soup, and unlimited wine. True the opportunity for time off or romancing was limited, and other than the family the Vendange was mostly blokes. Anyway in practice this did not matter much as although I was young, fit, with an eye for the ladies to be frank, the wine and exhaustion made thoughts of entertaining flirtatious conversation or even moments of passion a far less desirable desire than that of another ten minutes sleep. And after all this could last a few weeks at most and whilst still upright or nearly so there was yet more wine to be had, ad-in-vin-itum.

With each meal and especially the evening meal the life around 'the table' was a pleasure I'd not really encountered in my 'protestant' origins. My family had sat, not in complete silence but subdued with a rebuke "Robert, please be quiet at the table! whenever I started yapping away. Here meal time was more resembling an older children's party with jokes, tricks, demonstrations of half remembered poetry and song. All accompanied with traditional drinking games; these involving drinking yet more wine; this as the test, the forfeit and then the prize. Hey ho.

Predictably the wine did not improve our focus, but it sure made life jolly, often we would be singing and laughing in the fields as we worked. I have a deep bass voice and a repertoire of songs and when they found out I was soon doing requests, especially those of the Beetles. In return they'd sing, apparently humorous, French songs.

Each day the rows of vines marched on hour upon hour, day upon day, the repetition blurs, you start to dream picking grapes.
Then one day that farm was done, the work stopped and we all had to move on. I took a ride with a Breton to another farm nearby where we did another short stint. Similar here save the barn was smaller, the beds had more blankets and the horse was replaced by another inevitable grey Peugot pickup. This just like the others with faded mud splatted body was driven precisely, or rather imprecisely, maniacally the same. I remember the soup was better but the wine poor stuff compared to what I'd got used to.
As he drove us to the another town further north the Breton explained how by law they were supposed to give you wine, at least two bottles a day, and the two when you left, apparently the same as in the army. As wine was what these farmers made so it cost them nothing anyway. However human nature is predictable. Many farmers resented giving pickers their good wine, especially if it was valuable, so if they could sell theirs and replace it with a worse one for a fair profit...
He reckoned the better bosses wanted the best pickers and many thought these would do a better job returning over the years if they were

to drink what they made not some cheaper plonk. On those farms it was even more important not to pick it all fast, but to pick only the best, cleaning away any unripe or mouldy grapes, more so than we'd been doing. He said such places were where the wine was most valuable, and to be searched for as they looked after you better just so you would return. Less bread and more soup as he put it.

I was to be lucky. Though at first as so often in life it all started with misfortune when through an all to familiar circumstance my new Breton friend disappeared. Having taken my cash contribution to fill up he never came back to complete our journey northwards leaving me waiting in the café where I had just been treating him royally.

I slowly very slowly realised he was not returning and I was not going anywhere further, and worse, it was raining, torrentially. Fortunately through experience I had my most important items with me, he got my bag of dirty clothes (nice bag though, made it myself from carpet). But he had also got those bottles of wine the last two farmers had given me on leaving. (An excellent tradition as I note elsewhere.)

The café was closing so I wandered out and sheltered here and there between downpours, then decided I was best sitting it out till the next days dawn hiring at the Mairie.

This town was quiet. Of course normally everything shut each afternoon in the country, all day on a Sunday. Then during Vendange many folk went elsewhere to help family in the fields so most non-food shops would take a holiday.

The weather paused, the sun shone wanly so I set out and walked to the edge of town. The café might be worth re-visiting later that evening and the night might get interestingly raucous, but I needed a refuge until morning, preferably a dry one. Heading up into the hills, followed a lane then a track coming across a disused quarry part filled with dark water. Obviously used by hunters large numbers of shotgun cartridges littered the floor of a windbreak shelter come bird hide by the lagoon edge. I set up camp there with my wee tent and just in time as another heavy storm came over.

Now don't forget I was of my time and this was the mid Seventies so along with daily meditations and yoga I followed the Chinese I Ching book of changes. Carried the heavy tome with me everywhere along with my hand made yarrow stalks to throw the hexagrams for guidance. I still have the scrap of paper from that day in my copy with the marks for Sui/

Following becoming Tui/ Joyous. This image I cast while my clothes dried by the wee fire I'd kindled had seemed appropriate "Thunder in the middle of the lake, The image of following, Thus the superior man at nightfall, Goes indoors for rest and recuperation." Indoors seemed to stretch a point, the tent in the bird-hide which was hardly more than half a bus shelter, rest seemed likely to be uncomfortable as I had little to eat, and far far worse, I was realising to my chagrin and thirst, no wine.

Someone was shouting. I looked up at the rim of the quarry over the other side of the water where some folk, who'd presumably been picking grapes, were waving to me, I waved back. Thinking nothing of it I huddled closer to my smouldering fire for its meagre warmth for the dead wood I'd been forced to use was too wet. I dozed, to awake abruptly. A buzzing noise and coming down the track in the dusk was a Citroen 2CV van, the sole allowable farmers' alternative to Peugot pickups. (The Renault 4 outsold both in far larger numbers but was a townie car thought too tinny by farmers, more a car for those who only drove on metalled roads.) I was worried, having hiked and camped before and with the recent midnight fiasco in mind I guessed I was once again being moved on, indeed at best, for now being on my own other possibilities were coming to mind.

Anyway the driver seemed to be neither the law, nor a mugger, he was on his own and seemed friendly when I showed him my piece of card. He spoke in French, I obviously looked blank so he nodded and indicated to go with him so I grabbed my things and obliged, at least the van might have a heater.

He spoke very little English and I even less French so we drove silently some little distance through the damp countryside. It was very dark now, occasional lights sprinkled over the hillsides showed farms here and there. Some flashing past closer by and in a moment's glare we shot past a farmyard milling with folk and machinery. Our headlights turned sharply down a steeply winding track. We pulled into a farm courtyard set into the hill bounded on the lower side by yet another medieval barn. I made an educated guess, was that where I might be staying?

Bernard, as I later found his name to be, took me up the ancient stairs to a loft dormitory set out with rows of beds and indicated an empty one. Oh joy there were enough blankets, a bolster pillow and SHEETS, luxury. I left my bag and followed Bernard back down next door to 'the cave' where his team ('eekip' as I heard it) were just starting dining. Whereas on most farms the 'cave' might well have been a cellar it was often just a cool barn, here it was one of several tunnels cut back into the hillside. We went into this cave through huge doors opening from the courtyard. Down the middle ran large trestle tables with rough well worn benches. About two dozen or so folk were sitting on these, half of them with their backs to one wall. A couple of narrow side tables were clasping the other wall leaving just enough of a gap behind the opposite benches for food to be brought in and out. I was shuffled down to a place at the far end to be immediately poured a glass of wine. This wine tasted like nectar. I'd been sobering up since the night before, cold and wet all day and now there was a wonderful warm buzz all round, and a full bodied aroma smooth on my tongue, oooooh this was gooood wine. Life was looking rosy or should it be rosé?

I was given a chunk of bread and offered a green salad which I wolfed down, my bowl was then filled with soup, no sooner had I scoffed that than a dish of peas with tiny pieces of bacon was served, then mashed potato with thick aromatic gravy, then roast meats. This was bizarre, I seemed to have stumbled into a feast, I tried a piece of every dish. (Generally I avoided eating meat and would eat around it though not getting too upset at eating a modicum -especially if hungry.) One of the others demonstrated for me to clean my bowl with a piece of bread, I did so, to then be served a dessert of semolina and prunes. Then bowls of fresh apples and pears, and platters of cheeses were put on the table. This was heaven, and the wine was so wonderful I drank slowly, appreciatively.

No-one seemed to speak English well enough to converse, and it would have been rude, and impossible to have done so in the fracas. My French was, effectively incompetent as my friend, who was a language teacher, had put it. My problem is I do not hear words well, not even in English. It's a sort of auditory dyslexia where I mis-hear words, these seem lost in the flow not segregated and so hard to recognise and separate out. Basically I don't understand spoken French, or often even English, unless very clearly enunciated and even then I lip read much of the time. So though I could not understand spoken French very well rather bizarrely I could speak a simple Franglais, a mangling of Latin based words I knew from voluminous reading.

Regardless of my ability or lack it was near impossible to just chat to anyone for with the hub-bub all round the room, you had to almost shout. Later I learnt there were several very different versions of regional French; voices in Belgium French, Swiss French, Algerian French, as well as local Rhone, Lyonnais, St Etienne and Paris accents. I would have needed to be a great linguist just to talk with most of these folk. Still it did not matter, they were cheerful, friendly and expansive, it all seemed more a feast, a celebration than a simple meal.

Bernard stood up, went to the side table, came back with several dusty corked bottles and proceeded to open them carefully, wiping each cork with a cloth before using the ancient grapevine handled corkscrew. I was shown to empty my glass, and there was a hush. We were each given a fill, obviously this was special, was a toast coming? Bernard sipped his, as did we all. OH MY GOD the wine before had been wonderful, this exploded in my mouth, even more aroma, so rich, so full, so smooth, spirit legs ran down the inside of my glass showing me this was strong wine. Bernard said something and several people called out numbers, then he said something else and a number too fast for me to catch.

Then we were indicated to drink up, eat a morsel of bread and another fill from a second row of bottles. Once again we sip, it is the same supreme flavour, or is it, the same but not the same, more caramel though only subtly, more

body, even more legs. Again folks seemed to be calling out numbers.
Ah I get it, finally understanding it's guess the year, the vintage. Well what a good game another brilliant tradition. My head was reeling, suddenly Bernard was gone, the tables were cleared and games of cards appeared.
I leant back on the cold wall behind and breathed deep. Around me the room slowly turned, I shook my head, time to search for that bed. Looking around most of the others had already disappeared. I finished off my glass, my god, the flavour hit me again. Had I just stumbled upon that mythical paradise for grape pickers, a farm with incredible food and even better, superb wine! I slipped off, dog tired, I needed to sleep as I knew the morrow would be an early start and a hard days work for sure. The sheets were rough and delicious to slide into, I went out like a baby not waking till woken in the pre-dawn light.
Breakfast was just before dawn, in the cave again, and what a breakfast, as good a buffet as many a fine hotel. Soup, of course, and wine, coffee, hot milk, bread, butter, cheeses, ham, sausage, boiled eggs, bars of chocolate, fruits, bowls of home made apricot, raspberry and other jams. I was not sure where to start but ploughed in anyway.

Soon we were off, with a sir-pet and bucket apiece, to work some rows along the track on the way in. Same sort of grape vine training here as the last places, each bush tied up to its own stake, in ordered rows across the sloping fields. I was put to work next an older man who carefully showed me which grapes to leave as too mouldy or unripe, and he muttered 'fleuriste' if I let many leaves fall in my bucket. Though my skill was already well honed I found it hard to keep up with him for despite his age he was nimble and practiced. Every so often Bernard would come along the line to help but really inspecting our buckets, nodding and tutting as appropriate (never at mine of course).

I had not realised Bernard was that better viticulteur straightaway, indeed I did not even know he was the boss thinking he more foreman as he seemed too young. For some days I thought the older man I had been set to work with might be the boss. Turned out he was Bernard's father in law. A kindly man with bovine features and figure he spoke little English but would use simple French words slowly enough to get through to me. He taught me far more accurately than I had already guessed which grapes looked fine but were not quite ipe enough, or too mouldy (curiously some moulds are better or worse than others, and a little of some such as the 'noble rot' are not a huge problem), not to ever let any vinegary ones go in the bucket and that it's best to bury those. To be most careful not to pick bunches looking good but with brown withered stems as these were bitter, and most of all not to let many leaves fall in my bucket. There was a striking emphasis on quality here that was obviously higher than on other farms so far, and suited me. I'd rather loathed picking carefully as instructed when other pickers had been, lovely old word, lackadaisical, and put all their rotten bunches in with their good. Here that would not be wanted, nor tolerated. I liked the challenge.

I had already earned the difference between the original vine with an old established framework and all the young shoots springing from this. Seemed the frame endured year after year with all the young shoots being cut off each autumn. The frames slowly grew larger but then might be cut back to start re-building again. For sheer production the vines could be heavily cropped but then the quality suffered. The more shoots that grew meant more bunches of fruits, and leaving too many could then ruin them all. So a second pruning had been done in early summer retaining only some of the shoots to crop. The fewer shoots left fewer bunches but those of sweeter and cleaner berries. Some places before each vine was a thicket, a lot of crop produced but not that sweet or tasty. On this farm the vine frameworks were very hard pruned, you could see their history written in the joints and stubs each supporting fewer better spaced very open young canes producing mostly high quality grapes, smaller tighter sweeter bunches.

There was another improvement here, the jhzollo's oval barrel had been modernised into a glass fibre replica. However not fully understanding the sheer strength of glass fibre this baby bath had been made nearly as thick and heavy as the wooden originals. To further save effort and speed the rush to the vats he did not carry his jhzollo down to larger containers at the bottom of the row. Instead very large boxes were already up in the rows, also made in glass fibre, which with a simple frame and wheel could be picked up and wheeled down the rows straight up a ramp onto the waiting tractor and trailer. I could see how this would reduce the jhzollo's work saving his carrying so much weight so far and rather slowly, here the grapes could get to the vats even faster.

We were stopped by the cry of "Soupe" and there was a second breakfast in the fields. Everything was as generous as for the first breakfast, now spread out on blue and white chequered tablecloths. The early morning mists were clearing revealing behind us a green and brown chequerboard of fields dominated by a huge mound of a hill with a small church or chapel darkly silhouetted on the very top, Mont Brouilly. Little did I apprehend how I was to be under its spell for weeks every coming autumn. Not once or twice but annually over the next dozen years, amounting to more than six months in total solidly, stoically, slightly inebriatedly picking grapes.

We worked on till gone midday when again 'soupe' was called, we traipsed down the track to the courtyard where we washed out our buckets. (Another improvement, for grape juice was stickily lining them and in the warmth they otherwise soon became vinegary, better we cleaned them straight away than leaving them to be rinsed just before they were in use again.) We shuffled onto the benches in the cave but this time the end doors were fully open and in the fierce noonday light the hill of Mont Brouilly was now in spectacular view with its chapel blackly silhouetted on top.

Lunch commenced, again a plethora of wonderful French farmhouse food, much grown on the farm's own plot. Always a soup though not always bread but different each day, and always salads: endives, lettuce, shredded carrot and beetroot, tomatoes, flageolet beans and croutons, with chunks of those big rounds of bread I'd seen at the Boulangerie. Then came that idiosyncratic way the French had of eating their 'main course' in distinct parts with the potatoes and gravy separate to the vegetables and again from the meat. You could never be quite sure how many more dishes were to come and whether you should eat more of whatever was going.

Now as I said I was a pragmatic mostly vegetarian avoiding buying or choosing meat but not labouring the point, hitch hikers cannot be choosers. I'd also learnt the lesson from hitch hiking that it is better to avoid dietary arguments with anyone possibly willing to feed me. I did not much like most meat anyway so I found it simpler to avoid eating any large amounts or chunks but not getting too upset with gravy, stock or even the odd small bit of this or that meat on a pizza or in a sauce. Most of all I was compassionate to animals but not an intellectual abstainer, I had grown up on a farm and my semi-vegetarianism came from my dislike for commercial animal abuse and modern factory farming not from killing and eating an animal. I did not on the whole consider meat a heinous sin as such, just something I generally avoided buying or eating in quantity.

Which was fortunate as at that time vegetarianism was as alien to the French (and nearly as much to the British) as was sunbathing in the Arctic. I doubt any savoury dish, including every ostensibly vegetable one, was devoid of some sort of meat, though not in great quantity more as flavouring. Their peas came in a smooth creamy peppery sauce with shallots and just a few tiny pieces of bacon, sufficient to impart their essence, oh the aroma, the flavour.

One day Bernard's charming and thoughtful wife Eliane noticed I seldom ate the meat course as such and asked if I was Muslim or Jewish as she had thought I might be avoiding the pork. I explained, with gross mistranslational assistance from others, how I preferred not to eat much meat. "What none?" So I tried to explain my pragmatic but long winded position of how I most avoided factory farmed meat 'in chunks' though was less concerned where it was used for flavouring, similarly with fish or whatever. Somehow this all went awfully wrong for she determined I liked chicken. So as a kindness at the next meal she presented me with their finest chicken delicacy, a roast head and neck. I awkwardly declined as politely as I could manage trying to explain again I'd prefer no meat but would still eat dishes with some in, and they were not to worry. When pressed how did I stay strong without protein I explained I ate cheese and eggs, Aaaah, this at last made some sense to them- I was obviously an invalid on a bland diet. Of course, I'd suffered a 'crisis de foie', liver crisis. This seems a uniquely French syndrome finding existence as chronic indigestion brought about by excessively rich eating and drinking (that is I mean excessively beyond the normal meaning of excessively as virtually all French meals are intrinsically a tad excessive).

To be frank not Frankish, I simply don't want to eat much meat. If any I prefer it with vegetables luxuriating in rich sauces and dishes not on it's own, so huge slabs are simply not appealing. And if I must eat 'a chunk' I prefer it to be well done, very well done, ideally near charred not still bloody.

This prejudice for 'cooked' as opposed to 'rare' has often proved very English, and as near difficult to explain in France as vegetarianism. The term 'roasted meat' once transposed into French seems to mean a piece of raw meat that has been held near a candle flame just long enough to not actually risk cooking it. Pink and dripping may suit many folk but I was seldom ever tempted to try a second taste.

However I found I loved the 'jus' the gravy from the roasts, this soaked into morsels of bread was excellent.

I was not worried as I said, traces of meat were no huge concern and I loved tasting each and every dish even if I seldom ate much from those which were too meaty. This was such wonderful food, it was the grandmother who did almost all the cooking which was no mean task preparing a buffet picnic for the fields with three sit down meals for around two dozen or more people every day for several weeks. But of course years of practice made it routine. As the years came and went I got to recognise the sequences of dishes, each wonderful combination, and looked forward to almost every one even those great piles of roast meats.

I most adored the green beans, these were fried with onions and a few herbs in stock and I couldn't get enough, indeed this was one dish I managed to request any surplus to be saved for me for the next day. The pork mince stuffed tomatoes I found had too much meat for me but could donate that to another and just have the baked flesh, what a flavour from those huge beefsteak tomatoes, something I'd seldom seen in the UK. Souffles made with liver were another dish rather too rich for me but a small portion went so well with their 'kenn ell' in a tomato sauce. These were a local speciality, small white sausages made with Pike. Now I'd eaten Pike, my grandfather and I fished for it, horrible muddy flakes full of needle like bones. So I'd not have tried these if I'd known, however they were very nice, very very nice. One year I wanted to buy some to take home, going from shop to shop with little success until I realised why a) my French was so bad I could not explain what it was, ie fish sausages in a tin, and if anything was being proffered it was cinnamon ('kann ell') and b) quenelles were not common, quite a local delicacy apparently, eventually found some in a delicatessen supermarket.

The plethora of savoury dishes were followed by desserts: pear and apple tarts, flans, rice, semolina and sago with plums or apricots baked in or with dollops of jam, baked fruits, cakes and biscuits. Then fresh fruits: apples, pears and sometimes plums. And finally coffee and cheeses, including some 'krotts' which were hard dried goats cheeses, I got to love these as the perfect precursor to tasting the finer wines. Now from breakfast onwards this remarkably good wine was available by the bottle and in flagons in the fields. Too good to waste this was sipped at every opportunity, gorgeous. And as on that first night there was often a guess the year competition when even finer vintages from prior years to be tasted. Eventually I learned the years so well I could place them in order. However I could not understand how some nights I could get it so wrong, then one night when helping empty the vats I understood Bernard did not make just the one brew. He made several, these were then blended, but he kept some of each vat back and bottled these as his own 'super-specials'.

I got to understood just how good his wine was. He won prizes, usually the top prize, for the whole area frequently and his wine was apparently already 'sold' to Swiss merchants years before it was even picked! His meticulous culture of the vines, their multiple pruning, the neat effectiveness of his wine making, the care of the grapevines, then of the grapes, all was textbook. He had the best fields on the sunniest slopes of a major Cru, ie the terroire was perfect. His scrupulous hygiene impressed me, my grandfather had made cider and I remembered brushing bird droppings off while readying his antique wooden press with a quick hosing down…

We would start picking and throughout the day the grapes would be rushed to the cave to be broken up and started fermenting with a bottle of special yeast. Each day this would be repeated for ten days when there was even more work.

Now the first days' fermenting grapes were removed from the vats, the free liquids were run out and the mass of skins, pips and stalks dug out to be pressed in a most impressive machine! This was an age old design though made with modern materials and mostly stainless steel. The masses of grape residues were shovelled into a barrel shaped slatted drum. When full the ends were screwed inwards along a massive central bolt squeezing out their contents. The juice ran out of the fine slats and then the ends were run backwards as it unscrewed. And here was a most ingenious trick.

I have a small press, it's easy to get more juice, though of a lower quality, if you break up the packed down mass and re-press it. This is not easy as the pressed hard lump is not easy to turn back into wee bits until you first break it into manageable chunks. And this huge press produced a massive, solid, plug the width of the barrel. The cunning design was there were chains inside connecting the end-plates. These were no problem in the pulp just 'curling up'. Then when the plates were unwound the chains were pulled straight breaking up the mass most effectively. I was, as I noted, more than a little impressed.

Once re-broken up these pips, stalks and skins can then be re-squeezed, broken up and squeezed again, and even a second or third time (with the poorer quality juice going for 'economic' or weak table wine for everyday use.) Though as the old saying goes squeezed "But not hard enough to make the pips squeak". Exactly, for if the pips squeaked then they were ruptured and their bitter flavour would taint the wine. The terminally squeezed out pulp was sent off to a factory where it was turned into a brandy and animal feed. The still bubbling juice was carefully transferred to another vat until all fermentation had finished some months later when it was filtered and bottled.

Most red wines take a little longer to be drinkable than do white, Beaujolais is unique with its light red Nouveau drunk in the weeks after fermentation ceased. Better wines from Beaujolais take at least a year to be drinkable, several to be perfect, few go on getting better after a many years. Indeed one suspects it is then the rarity value that counts.

As the years passed I became a 'trusty' and was invited to help with many of the other tasks including the pressing. After experiencing this once I tried to avoid it, I like working in the fresh air not down in a cellar or worse inside a windowless claustrophobic vat. For although there was no longer the proverbial treading with the feet one still washed then stood in the grape mass as someone had to dig out the mass for pressing and clean down the vat ready for it's next load. Some wore rubber boots but it was considered these may taint a fine wine whereas scrubbed skin would not.

This was more physical labour at the end of a long day and also surprisingly dangerous work. The fermenting grapes give off carbon dioxide in vast amounts which carries vaporised alcohol with it forming a delicious smelling but deadly draught. If you get the chance to stick your head in a vat it really is amazing, breathing fruity wine flavoured air, full of alcohol vapour, but best not on your own. Seriously this work is dangerous, almost every year farmers or their workers are overcome and either collapse and hurt themselves, or plain asphyxiate, or worst fall into their vat and drown. This is more than a little concern to friends and family as obviously the vintage will be spoiled... I apologise, can't resist the jest, it is a big worry.

The method with a rich Red wine such as Bernard's was to ferment the mashed grapes, skins, pips, stalks and all. This extracts the colour and tannins from the skins and stalks (as the juice is usually clear though there are also Teinteurier grapes with red juice). Whereas a White wine is normally made from white / greenish grapes and their juice is nearly always extracted first then fermented on its own without all the bits. Thus white wine has less tannins than red, a major difference in their flavours. Naturally a Rosé wine is often made from rose' grapes but can also be had by pressing red grapes for their near clear juice which is then fermented. Anyway as I said the pressing did not start until the first fill had fermented sufficiently which took about a week and a half, ten days most years, quicker when warmer (though slower and cooler was preferred). Then the half fermented juice was run out of the vats before the remaining mass of bits had to be dug out and got into the huge press.

Now the juice squeezed out on the tenth day was called 'paradie', in translation paradise juice. With some of the sugar surviving while much alcohol has formed so the mixture has a full fruity vinous grape juice taste, it is delicious. My first time I drank rather a lot, greedily, unwittingly, just as everyone intended, a rookie error. As the sweet fizzing mixture hits your stomach the alcohol goes straight through to your blood. The warmth then kicks the yeasts into overdrive and they ferment all remaining sugars (now including your last meal) to alcohol fast. And faster still that passes through to your blood. More sugar ferments, and so does that sugar from your meals. Bubbles form, these create pressure, you bloat. So simultaneously you become outrageously drunk, distended and barometrically challenged, sporadically relieved with obscenely massive repetitive farting, barfing and burping.

The hangover is where the paradise name comes from, it is ironical, for sure not long after drinking it you are in hell. And you have to drag yourself out of bed early with the dawning...

Some years ago I was showing my photos of the Vendange. I seldom took photographs back then, they were relatively expensive but more because I had realised that with a camera one solely saw thro' it and ceased being immersed in the imminent world all round. I'd sat one morning under a most intricately worked ceiling in the Alhambra palace watching folk rushing past, each would snap, snap, snap, then say something like "Hey Joe will love this" and passed on to the next photo opportunity. Seldom did someone, stop stare and SEE. I learned to photograph in my head instead, an app we all have though it seems few ever open.

Anyway those photos of the Vendange; a friend remarked what a beautiful sunset going down over the hills, I replied that that was the dawn! No problem for me as I'm a lark, up before most folk all my life. Downside is the corollary, I fall off my perch earlier each night than everyone else. Indeed at college some thought I was into heavy drugs as so many nights I'd be found snoring in a corner of the room, bar or party. As you know night life only starts well after dark and falling asleep at ten in the evening does not impress. Indeed if I really wanted to be at such an event I'd go to bed at five or six, sleep, rise and go late. (This is good practice anyway, behave as Royalty; arrive last, leave first. As you enter make waves excusing your tardiness with "Sorry, had to extricate myself from X's do to be able to get here." More importantly never leave saying goodbyes, even worse is to admit you're tired/bored, just slip away and most will never notice your absence as they'll likely be intoxicated. I've been credited with playing piano all night when I'd already caught the last train home.)

Back to those photos, one time I did take photos was the year my brother came with me. Showing our results back home in the UK it was noted how his were so much better quality than mine. Sharply in focus, crisp and well framed. Whereas mine were blurry, shaky, fuzzy, double exposed, all over the place. Had my camera been damaged? No, somehow I took photos that looked remarkably like what I was seeing through my drunken eyes…

Now don't get me wrong, we were not picking grapes sodden drunk but we were well inebriated. Sure if you had joined us and drank the same amount alongside you'd likely fall over. But drinking wine while working hard in the fresh air and hot sun seems to have an enabling rather than debilitating effect even though much larger amounts than usual are consumed. I have no medical evidence but it feels as if after the first few days you start to burn the alcohol rather than running on sugar. You get a second wind and as long as you keep imbibing another glass or two each hour you can work more intensely. And, at six glasses to the bottle that makes about three bottles during the working day plus say another or couple more with the evening repast.

One year I took a friend, leaving school he had first worked for a brewery where he'd received free beer (honest that was traditional, even in the UK!), loved his drink and was well good at holding it. He decided he'd test his limit, he admitted to two bottles every day at home so started on three the day we arrived. Each day he aimed to drink another bottle, six glasses, more. Off to a flying start he found like me he was able to drink more while working in the heat so soon got to five bottles a day. It was the day after he drank seven going on eight bottles, that on the way to the fields the next morning he lost his breakfast off the back of the trailer while the tractor was dragging us up the hill. He claimed the motion had caused sea-sickness and it was not the wine! Not discouraged he was soon drinking again, though a tad more modestly. As I've remarked the problem is not so much drinking a lot of wine while you are working but reducing that level when you stop, to be frank it is addictive! I guess that is why they give you a couple of bottles as you leave; to keep you topped up till you are far away somewhere else. Anyway not every picker was drinking all the time, many drank enough to just keep 'happy' while toiling. Apart from young family and their friends at a weekend who imbibed but lightly there were also Muslims who did not drink wine. They were given their own flagons of fruit juice to drink and separate dishes at meals so they could avoid those with pork. There was a terrible mix-up one evening. An old Algerian guy who had worked for many years accidentally started eating from a dish of peas misunderstanding it was his pork free one but it actually was the one with bacon bits for the rest of us, when his arrived moments later. But too late for he had already eaten some, and on his plate had discovered a small piece of the bacon / ham this dish is flavoured with. He was distraught, inconsolable, desperate. The others explained he believed he would now be excluded from paradise as he had eaten pork, he really believed this and was seriously upset. We tried to reason how could he be guilty as he had eaten it unwittingly, surely that was not a sin. However it seems it was, his whole life was now wasted or worse. I never found out if he ever resolved this issue, seemed a bit harsh, still each to their own ways.

Other than this one awful mix up mealtimes were remarkably free of stress, so much good food so well cooked was provided and they were careful. When they finally understood my desire to be as vegetarian as was convenient they boiled eggs to give me an alternative to ham and sausage at breakfasts first and second. And added more chocolate, to eat with bread, their odd habit I'd now adopted.

I loved the food, coming from a farming family myself I knew how to cook English meals and appreciated the fresh home grown and local produce they were using. And I was eating really well cooked meals of such a more interesting cuisine. What is more folk enjoyed being at the table, it was a party. In England we just did not have this, it was unimaginable. A farmer, his family and friends all sitting and eating and drinking with all of their workers. Enjoying every meal together over a fortnight or more. And any one who came by anywhere near any meal time was also invited / obligated to stay and join in. Late one morning two gendarmes arrived at our field. All our papers had been submitted as required by Bernard -and turned out one of us was wanted for an outstanding court case. The guilty guy was very roughly stuffed into the back of the police Renault and they were about to drive off when Bernard called 'soupe' and invited them to lunch. They were not slow. Immediately their pillbox hats came off they were as jolly as the rest of the team at the table and had a heartily good lunch, eating, drinking, laughing and joking with us all. However the moment they put their 'kipu' hats back on they became officious again. The offending guy was taken off with them for interrogation, but at least he had a full stomach. Every meal was an event and some days we even had a celebration as well (more cake and more wine) for someone's Saint's day. Now apparently in France at the time you could only (church or officially, never grasped which?) be given an allowable name from a list of approved names, which effectively meant it was one of the Saints. What is more one's true birthday was kept private while one was celebrated by friends and acquaintances on one's Saint's day instead. And there were plenty of Saints, many for every day of the year it appeared. This is a sensible idea as one has to discover and remember someone's birthday but the Saint's days are obvious. I won a surprise myself, I call myself Bob, for Robert, September 17th was St Robert's day according to their local calendar and so fell in the middle of the Vendange many years. So we all had an excuse and could have yet another toast of just a little more wine.

Most days we ate breakfast in the cave, the second in the field and then back to the cave for lunch and dinner. But on some days we were far from the farm such as when picking father-in-law's or brother's fields as there were many small family holdings in the area. On those days if not a picnic we would be taken to the grandparents in their 'workshop'. I guess this had once been a coach house for the building was old and rather ornate, the doors were large and opened onto a yard. So 'French' was this that as all the team were sitting at the table within the workshop they had a bee line of sight of the unisex toilet arrangement a few metres across the yard. This small half boarded shelter was of the old fashioned hole in the ground variety so one half hid behind the half boarding only just managing decency from their view, while one hoped bodily noises were covered by the general hubbub of everyone else at their meal.

The joy of this old workshop was the tools. The walls and roof were hung with countless tools, some so festooned with cobwebs and dust they seemed to have melded with the background. Many tools were for rustic carpentry or gardening and instantly recognisable, with some of curious agricultural heritage for tasks not immediately discernible. Some were obvious such as hammers, saws, scythes, forks and spades but the sheer diversity and number of others were perplexing. By their shiny handles and lack of cobwebs some were still in use but many were so dusty and webbed I guessed they had been hanging since before the last war, I later found out this was indeed so.

There were some curious tools for working willow withies, a compression wheel you fed them through so they would be squeezed and become more pliable. Other tools I gathered for making the barrels and trugs. This was almost a museum, however at the time there was no interest in such a treasure trove of antiquity.

Set to one side in a corner of the yard stood a temporarily evicted two wheeled tractor. This peculiar piece of antique machinery was allowed to pollute the atmosphere with a blue cloud once or twice a year when trugs of grapes needed moving from a couple of small fields which had particularly steep and difficult access. Not only did this weird machine pull a small trailer almost anywhere, but where the path was too narrow for even it to go it also had a winch underneath. A wire was unwound down the rows and trugs pulled back up on a sledge. Ingenious.

Over the years I got to know the various fields and enjoyed returning to each especially the smaller eccentric ones tucked in behind cottages and on odd ridges. In many you might catch the sound of the town bell striking the time but most were often wonderfully quiet (save for the occasional protesting Peugot pick-up in the distance). The views when you raised your head for a breather were so varied, gorgeous, and panoramic.

This mad practice of planting vines clinging to the slopes was because the vines make better quality grapes with less disease on higher and sloping ground. Thus the vine fields are positioned as high on the slopes as possible even though yields might be larger down in the damper bottoms. So you can often be well placed to see one way across the beautiful hills of Beaujolais, or out towards Switzerland across the Rhone valley laid out way below. Though to be honest most of the time you kept your head down and concentrated on the picking.

Now I remarked on how safe the sir-pet was as a knife, even so it was possible to cut yourself with the tip. This became thin and sharp as the acid juice ate it away, some would rub this on a stone to blunt it but it would soon return. And although the vines had no thorns they did have snags and stubs which could exact a nasty little wound as you caught on them. After a week or so your hands, and sometimes if you were clumsy, legs, resembled road maps with scratches and scars aplenty. However these seldom got infected as grape juice is a powerful antiseptic. The tannins in the grape skins could also turn your hands brown faster than the sun so your road map of scars could appear as if printed on old parchment.

Sunburn was a potential problem because of the long hours and theoretically the heat even more so. Though the Vendange is in mid to late autumn the heat could be incredible and some years after a long drought the rocks would be hot even into the night. I have no problem with heat though, love it, function better, just drink more and keep my hair wet or my head covered. Others were not so happy, surprisingly those from hotter countries seemed to cope with the heat less well than those from colder ones. I guess it is much to do with attitude, and common sense. As someone so aptly put it no such as thing as bad weather just bad clothes, and the same in the sun. Loose clothes, hat and lots of water inside and out. Anyway as I said earlier compared to plucking rotting spuds from half frozen mud with near frostbitten fingers this was a dream.

Conversely there were sodden wet years. These were no fun, we could not pick in heavy rain as the water on the grapes diluted the grape-juice, so we were held 'in barracks'. Now they still provided food, but less generously than when you were working, and wine, still plenty, so days off were spent drinking and intellectual pursuits, well cards. Then if it stopped raining you had to drag yourself into whatever wet gear was available and start picking. This was miserable work, the bunches tended to be huge, and mouldy, the vines uncooperative and the soil stuck to your willies (I brought my own boots, indeed for many years I kept my suite of Vendange gear in Bernard's barn rather than bring them up and down.

Worst about damp weather was the wet made the work more dangerous as it became far too easy to slip with the knife and or foot. These years the work could drag, and as the crops were heavy these were also the years when extra work could be had for days after the wine harvest picking the surplus for pressing as grape juice. A bit of a mixed blessing, the extra work and pay were welcome but meant continuing in grim conditions. But naturally grandmother helped supplying jugs of hot coffee and soup to keep us going.

Grape picking is serious work but of course some will mess about, aggravated by the stupidity the drink contributed to some. I detested those who would lob a bunch of grapes at you for fun. This was not often painful unless causing you to cut yourself of course, but it was unpleasant to have the sticky juice and squashed grapes getting down inside your gear. I found massive retaliation was the easiest way to stop this. Having noted the offender I would amass a half bucket pile of mouldy grapes, then when they were off guard I'd scoop up then deposit the lot over them. This gave me a reputation, and I could get on with the job unmolested.

However there was a local tradition that at the end of the last day there could be a grape fight, and that was just fun, you were going to shower and wash everything anyway. I remember the year I took my brother I heard the rumblings as the afternoon lengthened. With my dim understanding I gathered they were planning a patriotic combined attack of a dozen French upon us the two Brits. The odds of six to one against did not look good, so summoning up my best French, and years of back-history, I negotiated a secret deal, this changed the odds to thirteen to one, which looked a whole lot better.

As the final hour picking approached I readied myself leaving little piles of mouldy bunches ready to scoop into my bucket. When "FINIS" was called I scooped up the piles and moved rapidly up hill, as did the others, leaving my brother standing puzzled for a moment in the rows down below us. We turned round, we must have appeared formidable, uphill and a dozen to one. The exchange commenced. I did not need pelt him myself, the others were doing plenty enough, but I joined in anyway… My brother was seemingly not much amused by my treachery even though it was all in such good fun.

Of course some years there were not enough surplus grapes or poor quality bunches left over to waste on a fight. And even less often in those wet years there might be a massive surplus. Naturally grapes can be squeezed for their juice to be drunk fresh or processed rather than fermented. Normally the grapes from somewhere with the right terroir such as Beaujolais are worth more when turned into wine. However each wine's quality control limits the total amount of wine that is allowed to be made each year and means most farms can end up with a small surplus of grapes that are not wanted. Obviously those will be left from the least favoured fields. In some unusual years the excess is so great the farmers are allowed to sell these expressly for juice. Seldom would Bernard have enough surplus from his choice fields most years so more often we went to pick those of his family or neighbours with less favoured terroir. What different picking this was, the quality control was less enforced, it was just pick as much as fast as possible, certainly put me off buying grape juice ever since, worse I can taste the mould in most. Invariably these were great bloated bunches hanging on vigorous leafy vines so were hard work and heavy going. Your bucket filled so fast it was hard for one jzhollo to cope, another helped, then the choke point was the transport to the factory as much further than to the farm cave. It was a long drive with a tractor and overloaded trailer to a local co-operative with a long return back which risked the next batches of grapes sitting too long. I was taken to see the cooperative which was modern and hue with the same sorts of equipment, just on a much larger scale. Our grapes were sampled and weighed in and we rushed back for the next load already waiting.

Vine culture and wine making was so interesting, not the cows, spuds and sugar beet farming I knew. As each year passed I got to further understand and love vines, and viticulture, and all while wonderfully wined and dined, lodged in the most charming and beautiful surroundings.

As I'd noted a strange feature of the landscape was how few birds there about compared to back in England at that time. I slowly postulated they'd shot and eaten them, for whenever any bird was seen it was pointed at. And not with a one-finger-pointing arm but with an aiming-a–gun-pointing, and this done universally simultaneously by almost all the pickers. Some also intimating with fiddling-fingers-in-smacking-lips that many small birds were delicious tucker.

Oddly there were sometimes asparagus plants amongst the vines and I was told the orangey red berries were to fob off the birds. Now I know asparagus seeds are seldom eaten at home by birds so that's a red herring. Anyway I doubt even uncountable flocks of birds of Biblical plague proportions could have dented the grape production on so many thousands of acres all ripening at one time. No I reckon there really were few birds, they'd either accidentally or deliberately decimated and eaten their avian friends.

But then who am I to cast stones, I grew up in a farming, shooting & fishing culture, my grandfather even used to enjoy sparrow pie. It's just we still had great numbers of wild birds in the UK, in this region of France they seemed really really scarce. Evidence mounted as when asking what some coloured marks and signs on the tracks meant was told they were for the hunters and shooters –and this was not wild boar, deer or even rabbit country...

My fears of the birds having ended up in the kitchen were confirmed when I heard the story of a journalist who had been on manoeuvres with some French army squaddies in Guiana, S. America. While they were away from camp 'helping' the natives he spied a 'Wildlife of S. America' guide, with the time to read he noted some of the animals and birds had stars next to them. When the squaddies returned he asked who was so interested in nature-spotting various critters. They replied quite enthusiastically and not at all embarrassedly that these were not the critters they had spotted but those they had shot, cooked and eaten...

On conversing with one old man who had fled to England in the Second World War and had seen the number of wild birds we had. He reckoned it was the deprivations and starvation of the wars that had caused the decimation of so many birds in France. In fact he did not understand why with such tight food rationing we had not eaten ours, listing several he considered good tucker. Although he did not admit it as such I suspect from the way he talked that he may have had more than a few to help his rations while in the UK.

Perhaps this is the right place for revealing one of my more humorous episodes; well they all laughed at me! One of the endearing features of Vendange was then already dying away, it was the singing of traditional songs in the fields. In the manner of sea shanties these held work to a rhythm. Was eerie sometimes catching a faint rendering drifting through those misty hills.

Of course more often someone would be singing or humming a pop song, even occasionally whistling (does anyone ever now?). Well when they caught me singing along it became request time particularly for Beatles numbers. I was happy to oblige as I enjoy giving voice and naturally believe I am a superb baritone/ basso profundo with a bell-like counter–tenor range on top. I did have a large repertoire which I was happy to repeat. It was better singing after meals in the cave where it resonated, particularly as I could hit it's fundamental making it throb which

was impressive. When they responded with their favourite songs I would sing along when I could, anyway back to my banana skin event.
As you must have gathered by now my linguistic skills were erratic. Thus when I volubly and whole heartedly joined a rendition of Edith Piaf 'la vie en rose' (translating as 'life in the pink') they were all immensely and I mean immensely, amused with some creasing up in laughter, hearing my barbaric pronunciation as 'la viande rose' (translating as red meat).
So many were my gaffes!
French is not made easier by the number of common homonyms (words sounding similar such as vein, vane and vain). I've already mentioned my confusion of cannelle for quenelle but both those words are seldom used. Much more frequent in daily use were words revolving around the 'mare' and 'mure' sounds: apparently written as mer, mere, merde, and mieux, murs, mures, meilleur. I kept getting things so wrong. However unwittingly this made me a great wit at times with bon mots such as coming from England, across the Merde du Nord…
Of all my school subjects, other then Sport, I was poorest at French. So in an effort to improve my French my parents had arranged lessons with a retired teacher back in Eye. This was spooky as his home was musty, dusty and dark (sadly,

because he had lost his eyesight he needed no light). These evening sessions failing to improve me so other lessons were arranged with the school's assistant foreign student. Nowhere near so forbidding, nor unwelcome as I soon had a crush on her though she was of course a couple of years older. She lodged with some folk running a wool & knitting shop between the school and my home, also much more convenient as I did not have to cycle over to Eye. She was so patient, I would try, try and try to understand. I could read and write French badly, and my East Anglian accent and dialect did not help my pronunciation yet it was hearing what was said I had trouble with. Just found difficulty grasping the words from the sounds. I was not much different with some folks' English oddly finding it easier to lip read rather than listen. Anyway we spent hours trying to get me up to speed and that summer we went for cycle rides talking solely French, well trying. One afternoon we rode to see the old family farm where I had been born. Sitting on the 'meadow' once the front lawn of my now empty home we were noticed by my uncle driving past. He reported to my parents he had spotted me there with a girlfriend. My mother gushed "No, no she's not his girlfriend she's his French mistress."

If only! Still, despite all my efforts, and her patience, my use of French remained weirdly unbalanced. You see as I noted I could slowly read simple French and also put together sort of understandable sentences myself using my huge library of Latin based words, I just seldom understood their answers. After a few years floundering every time I went picking in France I took action. I enrolled for French evening classes during the winter (and also for Touch-typing as I was already writing and needed to do so much more speedily. This was one of my luckier decisions, the class was one guy, me and twenty young ladies, the shooting fish in a barrel metaphor comes to mind, ah happy days.) The evening classes helped a little but ineffectually mainly because of the equally misleading sounds coming out of the other students also burdened with strong local accents. So I raided the library were there was not exactly a plethora of books on French or any other language. I found but one 'French as she is spoken', which I took home without closely examining and started methodically to learn from that. Shame I did not look at the publishing year- it had been written way back when Queen Victoria was still a bit of eye candy. Thus I returned to Beaujolais that following autumn reciting such erudite phrases as "Cette vin c'est le bon Dieu en cullottes du velours." (This wine is the good Lord in velvet trousers.) Which was a bit like a spud-picker back in Norfolk quoting Shakespeare and Chaucer...

Amazed as they were at my utterances the lie was given when I still could not understand their speech when rapid. Mind you they appreciated my efforts, well laughed with me. Of course over the years I did learn to speak French more accurately, that is with a pronounced provincial Lyon come St Etienne accent (large towns from where the most pickers came). Even so I still could not understand anyone talking back at full pelt. But then as we all were so often a bit drunk then repeated repetition was not unusual anyway.

I was so pleased when finally I was able to make a joke, well a pun, in French, though with only faint enthusiasm from my audience as I guess it was probably about kindergarten level- Vendange, c'est un bien Raisin d'etre.

I mentioned earlier how I had learned to adopt a Scots persona when travelling in France or Spain, as this provoked a better welcome than being English. Well one year a genuine Scots guy turned up at Bernard's, spoke as little French as I'd started with so I helped out with explanations and so on. He was a good picker in terms of enthusiasm just could not get the quality control aspect right. And boy could he drink, no problem as I said, as long as you kept working. But he did have a slight problem which was a hefty dose of paranoia, which became a self fulfilling prophecy.

He would keep asking me / telling me that the other pickers were talking about him, which inevitably soon led to them actually talking about him. As my French was never good enough to capture rapid conversations I could not tell what happened but somehow someone got offended and the Scots guy had no idea of what it was they were saying about him but sure got the idea they were talking about him. His paranoia fuelled reaction was shouting at them, which of course led to pushing, and shoving. And thank goodness the boss intervened or it would have been a right brawl, anyway the guys all calmed down. That night at the table he said he'd be off as he 'wasn't welcome' -which had been entirely his own making as as I had said the Scots were always welcome. He had worked up a problem when there had been none, all he'd overheard was folk chatting in a language he did not understand. If he'd not been paranoid he'd have found them friendly. I certainly did despite my being a square pin at least initially, I was forgiven my not understanding things, such as where one sat at the table. (Close to the boss were the prize places, at the extremes were for children and visitors. In between depended on your seniority in the eekip.)

A major difference between France and England is when folk get together and without arrangement sing or perform. Too often here in Blighty we criticise, carp and denigrate others' efforts. There at the table one was praised for the effort, and pleasure taken despite the odd stumble or flat note. And as I said they were forgiving of my blunders as I was a 'stranger' to their customs.

One thing I found awkward was the physical intimacy of their greetings, and the frequency, it took me years to get used to their less formal formal ways. Now being English I am already emotionally restrained from any form of contact, the notable exception of a handshake is done at full arms length, at tilt, briefly. In France they don't just grab your hand but the whole arm, then sometimes man-handle this into hugging you like a bear. And the social kiss of a peck on the cheek was manifold and confusing with when, where, which, how many?

I sort of coped with this French penchant for handshaking, but could never forecast their timing or rather the correct inter-mission period. Okay at the start of a meeting, or a new day you shake every hand, seems obvious, but to do so again after a trip to the next farm, or just after a long lunch... Sometimes I wondered whether I should shake every hand after a prolonged absence at the toilet...

Eventually having become so used to this physical greeting and returning to my parental home I forgot to re-adjust to suitable English distant reticence, and hugged my father who panicked, it seemed to him this meant I had turned 'queer' as he put it while I was away? So sad.

Another notable difference is the way the French grape pickers formed a team (ee-kip), there was a moulding together I'd not witnessed before in England. Perhaps because I'm not too desirous of immersing myself. Many Brits are staunchly individual, so are the French, but there they seemed less burdened by what you did for a living. Far more important were the rules of The Table where each takes their part, points apparently awarded for skill, intellectual achievement and entertainment value as much as wealth or status. And they had a coming together to make things work for everyone in a way I had to admire.

A fine example was the year when quite unusually a female student joined us band of blokes. Now in England this would have resulted in the alpha males posing and strutting, in-

fighting and general discontent as many men vied for her attentions. Not in France it seemed. The first day I kept hearing odd conversations I just could not get a hold on, nothing unusual there. But you're just sure they were talking about you, dismissed as paranoia. Then there was a meeting that night in the main barn dormitory, they insisted I stayed awake if not sober and attend. They explained to me what was going on. Still not getting it, they explained with more frankness, appropriately through an Italian translator. They wanted me to court, seduce or at the very least accompany this lovely girl. "You know, as you say, chat her up!" What! Now I was not usually unwilling to enjoy female company, far from it, and I was happy to sit next anyone at table and to work alongside anyone in the fields if that would please. But I needed to understand what the heck was going on.
Slowly and carefully thro multiple translations it was explained it was my privilege /duty as the 'guest/ foreigner' at the table to occupy her one way or another so she would be put 'out of play'. With her no longer to be vied for this would then free up all the rest of the guys to get on happily drinking and working together again. The team would work. I not un-reluctantly agreed. Poor girl, she was unfortunate and could speak English, so ended up 'enjoying' my droning on in

a James Joyce-an way at four or more bottles to the wind each and every all day long…

Most years though as noted the harvest was picked predominantly by a bunch of men with only the occasional wife or girlfriend, and of course at weekends the whole extended visiting family. I like the company of women as the conversation is often better but in French that would not be not easy, and I was a bachelor so could have a love interest, but the Vendange was but once a year so I'd forget about the ladies for the duration It was plenty busy enough picking grapes, eating, drinking, and then most definitely sleeping. It was not the spirit was not willing it was the body was exhausted, and to be frank, simply too drunken. Anyway, very soon we'd soon be finished and off to town looking well fed, well tanned, and with cash in our pockets.

Indeed Romance could wait.

Though one year I fell head over heels for a French student on the last day, and then lost her so utterly foolishly.

We had nearly finished picking the usual fields and had only a day to go when Bernard asked us whether we wanted another days' work, another farm needed a hand. Not unusual and np problem for most of us though some already had their travel booked. We set off the next morning on the tractor and trailer, as we travelled we passed several places I'd expected us to stop. Then we turned into a long drive up to a grand dilapidated chateau. I had seen this so often in the distance over the years but never got near, it had a strange aura. Almost derelict we were ushered into what had once been a modest ball room, most evidently this had recently been housing chickens, it was now where some other pickers were finishing breakfast to which we were naturally expected to help ourselves. With much hand shaking, even for France, it was very friendly.

As we were waiting I wandered out to inspect a large array of beehives I'd noticed outside. I had my own bees and was curious, especially as to the arrangement and size of the boxes. Two girls called me over saying I should stay away as the bees had been upset and had stung one of them recently. We started chatting and continued as we went off picking. The day flew by, we got on well, and though her English was no better than my French, it did not matter, we seemed to understand each other well. Stopping for lunch a convoy descended to the grandparents' yard where trestle tables and benches were set outside to cope with so many. It was so festive, the last day was always celebrated but perhaps because of the greater number this was more raucous.

We returned to a shortened afternoon of work as our many hands had near finished picking the crop clean. Soon we were told to be getting ready to leave. I told Bernard I would like to stay and walk back later, it was no more than a few miles. He seemed upset and was I sure as I'd miss the last night party he'd planned. I gave in, said a hurried goodbye, to the student, she seemed to be only a little upset at parting, indeed seemed to regard it almost humorously as I got reluctantly on the trailer. I was a bit sad that evening, it was last night so poignant anyway. I washed and changed and went down to the cave, where surprise surprise, everyone was waiting, including her and her friend. Bernard, and everyone else, had noticed how we had got on. So he had invited them to his party before we left then driven back to get them. It was wonderful, the food was fantastic, his wines flowed even more with so many specials from individual fields. Then I made my mistake. I loved the wine so much I had seldom drunk the super strong home distilled spirit splashed about on these nights. This 'oh-duh-vee' was almost odourless and very very potent. So besotted and entranced was I by my company I did not keep my hand over my glass and before I could notice I had been 'topped up'. A legitimate 'game' when done with wine but not spirit, this was an evil trick as before another hour the ohduhvee had me on my back looking up at the night sky. I had been carried out unconscious having fallen over whilst dancing.

It was late the girls were leaving, I dragged myself up embarrassed and confused, tried to talk but had to turn and be awfully ill in front of them. As they got into the 2CV she beckoned, I lurched over, she gave me a tissue. I wiped my face, my lips, my chin then dropped it in a nearby rubbish bucket. She looked aghast, drew back and they drove off. I went to bed with the dawning that somehow I'd messed up. The next morning with a hangover like never before I sat forlorn at breakfast. Several were like me nursing their heads, some few were fine. All seemed amused and curious. Eventually a tri-lingual Italian explained. Everyone had seen how the Englishman had chemistry with this girl, they had all expected a great romance, at the party everything had been going swell but then at the end I'd acted so strangely.

I just did not understand. He explained "She stayed with you as long as she could after you got stupid drunk, they had to go, she wanted to give you her name and address so you could write her and meet up. She wrote it on a paper serviette and gave it to you, and what do you do? You spit on it then throw it away. Why?"

They say it is better to have loved and lost, I guess so.
However life moves on and after each picking finished just as each other year I would leave to return home or move on to pick elsewhere. When many years had passed I became a family friend welcome to stay another day or two. I loved bicycling and Bernard would lend me his so I could explore the region. It is staggering how far you can travel in a days cycling on the flat such as my native East Anglia, and how much less far you can ride amongst steep hills such as those of Beaujolais. My word the scenery was delightful and although I can find little other praise for French driving I must say they generally allowed more room to bicyclists than on English roads, if they saw you that is. Bernard's farm was in the Burgundy region, a Beaujolais. There is a vaunted race each year to get the newly made 'Beaujolais nouveau' to London as fast as possible. Bernard's wine was not of that ilk, but one of the finer sorts, made to be drunk within a few years though not immediately nor beyond say seven. Within a few hours you could cycle through a dozen famous wine making villages. Each area and wine has an appellation, this has to be grown on the specific village's fields. Bernard's was Brouilly, one of the finest as I said, along with Fleurie, Moulin-a-

vent, Julienas and Morgon, all close nearby. Cycling was hard work, up and down, but the rewards of scenery, and stopping for a taste of wine, impeccable. Further afield towards Macon the land was flatter and the wines were lighter, mostly red though with one remarkably fine white, Pouilly-Fuisse. Introduced to this by Bernard I enjoyed that as a change from my diet of red.

One of the notable differences with home, other than the terrain and lack of birds, was the state of the buildings. In England huge efforts are made to 'gentrify' the appearance, make the building look newer, more valuable, while sometimes inside is not quite so delightful. Here exquisite worn shabbiness was everywhere, the outside of a building could be apparently derelict though it was often chic inside. I was told the way their tax laws worked made it expensive to have a renovated appearance outside so that was kept 'impoverished'. Meanwhile inside, especially the kitchen, would be modernised and no expense spared on the cooker and fridge. Many homes had little wallpaper and more often plain paint, less carpets than in England and more bare floors. Oddly most every window and door was fitted with a grill, substantial shutter or similar. It seemed break-ins were or presumably had been much more of a common threat.

The shops in the small towns had similar aged appearance, old cafes, old bakeries, old butchers, all looked much the same as on postcards of these places from half, even a century before. One sensible arrangement many shops still had was the separation of cash and food. You requested whatever from some grumpy old woman or man who served you, and then you paid another, grumpy old woman, who sat in a separate booth. I applaud this as having repaired arcade machines I know just how filthy nasty dirty coinage is, notes may be as bad. It really is disgusting to handle money then food with the same unwashed fingers.

On the other hand so to speak the French toilet was also often something to be considered as a lesson in medieval plumbing. I mentioned one at the grandparents' yard which was rustic in the extreme, many were similar, often with a jug of water added, sometimes a stick, presumably for prodding reluctant items through the wee hole. At Bernard's he'd sensibly constructed a composting toilet, effectively water less. This was set on a slope, you had a door at the top in which was a bottomless toilet with seat, everything dropped into the lower part which was stuffed with hay, straw and leaves. This mass was retained by a removable barrier accessed further down the slope. Eleven months after we had finished it was well rotted and dug out ready for our next onslaught. Admirable in efficiency and effectiveness, but my word you can hardly imagine the humming perfume that hit you when it was in regular use. This had the effect on your nasal membranes of a tear gas attack. Closely followed by your body evacuating as rapidly as possible under this prompt, or maybe was it the clenching of ones breath. Constipation seemed alien to the Vendange as Vegetarianism. Indeed the joke was the bosses did not mind feeding you as much as you wanted as you gave it back to them as valuable manure sooner enough. In the fields we did as the bears, remembering to go where we had picked not were about to! Grape leaves are not bad toilet paper but being a country boy I looked for mulleins and dead nettles with their softer leaves.

The cafes and bars had an odd arrangement with the cubicle for the ladies set beyond the troughs for the men which was a bit startling when a woman came through while you were in full flow. Oddly the shabby ancientness of these facilities together with paranoia whilst using them was strangely reminiscent of my old school.

Disgustingly something I had to have explained to me was why so many walls in towns had the bottommost yard or so of a streaky darker shade than above. This was thanks to innumerable drunken men caught short and turning to the wall for some imaginary camouflage. (I am surmising here, it is possible some women might pee onto a wall but I presume they prefer to squat somewhere.)

To reduce this ubiquitous public hazard some towns erected pissoirs in the market places, indeed there is the famous story of one in Clochemerle (translates as 'petty parochial squabbling') which in reality was the nearby village Vaux-in-Beaujolais which I visited to use as my convenience on many of my bicycle tours. Quite predictably this has become a tourist attraction.

Surprisingly with so many competitors the direst dunny I ever had to visit in France, was in the basement of a Parisian tenement. Without doubt the building was originally medieval and had been built about and upon but never modernised since. This shared pit was timbered about with wood that bore indelible stains of its history, there was a cobbled floor and a festering hole which one feared may give way plunging you into a pit of god knows what underneath. (Though to be fair this was a shining example of hygiene compared to the khasi in Spain awaiting the ferry from Algeciras for Ceuta on the African side. This abomination appeared to have had a bomb of turds exploded within leaving no surface un-splattered or bedaubed.)

I love France for these eccentricities, which of course are normal to them, and they regard ours likewise. But I believe we may all agree on the frenetic nature of French driving or random duelling as it should be known. I travelled by many means to get to and from Beaujolais, and the most memorable / scary ones are always those in cars driven by French folk. To the age of thirty I had been in a half dozen car accidents where the car was written off, only one with myself driving, the other five were in France as a passenger.

I said French driving was effectively duelling, one year I was hitching to Bernard's and was getting nearer as I recognised the villages. It was not as slow hitching as it could be as the locals were expecting useful strangers anyway. I was picked up by a guy in a Renault4 van, I worked out from the gear in the back he was probably an electrician. We were haring along the winding roads with the usual Gallic insanity when in a narrow section we saw a bus coming towards us. Both played chicken till the last second panic brake, and both slowed down to a near stop barely metres apart. Eyeballing each other they kept pushing on relentlessly though either could easily have stopped. We met bumper to bumper over-rider, a mere bump of no account, but then neither would back up. From their seats they harangued each other through their windows, each wanted the other to reverse, each demanded total and instant capitulation, insulted each others face, nose, mother, habits. To be frank as an unbiased observer it was a difficult call: most definitely it's physically a harder job for the bus to reverse, but the road behind my driver was a long long way back to where we both could pass. I was surprised how long it was going on for, and the people on the bus mostly seemed to be enjoying the drama. I took my bag, said bye and slipped out of the car then slid past the bus and trekked on. Oddly the Renault never drove past me later, I still wonder what happened, did he turn around, or were still there eyeball to eyeball at nightfall?

Now as a hitch hiker I had become well used to stepping up and covering long hauls so it was no problem to march the lanes through the rolling countryside to Bernard's, I recognised the villages and worked out I'd be there by dusk. Luckily I was saved the last few miles being spotted by Bernard on his way home from the

Boulangerie with a basket of warm bread, what a delightful 'home-coming.

Bernard was quite a handyman, had to be as a farmer, but oddly claimed not to understand the workings of a car. It seemed this was not uncommon in France where possession of the correct paperwork seemed more important than actual skill. Certainly my fixing aility appeared near magical to them as I did not have a proper 'mechanics certificate'. One lunch we had come down from fields, us on the tractor and trailer and Bernard in the 2CV. We finished lunch and sat inside the cave as it was showery weather. Bernard got in the 2CV van and spun the engine, spun the engine, again, again, it began to stink of petrol. He was yelling to his wife that the battery was flat, he was out of petrol, it was caput. All of which were manifestly incorrect. The battery was doing a Herculean job, and I feared the enclosed courtyard and cave would explode in a petrol fume powered fireball. He was then frantically trying to call for help on the phone, dialling number after number jabbering away. Then it was head in hands, everyone was busy, no mechanic, maybe not tomorrow either, nor possibly even the next.

I suggested I might be able to fix the car. With help from many translators I countered his protestations I was not qualified, how could I possibly be of any help?

Promising not to do anything just to look I lifted the bonnet. A 2CV is simple, as simple as you can get, though being a French design, odd. I knew a) there was electric power as engine turned, b) petrol as the air stank, c) it had worked an hour or so before, d) it was wet, wet, wet with puddles thus an ignition problem was likely, indeed very probable at he high voltage, spark, end rather than with the low voltage supply. Logically the fault could be: oily then flooded plugs, wet leads or plug caps, or damp in the distributor (which was a wee rotary switch, the contact breaker, for the spark sending it to alternate plugs in turn). Actually although everything had been drenched with mud the engine being warm had dried somewhat overall. The leads looked fine, they led down to the distributor which I found down under the front of the engine. As a motorcyclist and amateur engineer I must say the economy and simplicity of fitting it there is far outweighed by the guarantee that it will get splashed too often. So to make this even more fallible the cunning designers had ensured the innards were only protected by a really flimsy plate, and inadequate gasket.

When Bernard looked away for a moment I took the opportunity and loosened this cover, dirty water seeped out.

I cried in glee pointing out to Bernard this was the probable cause and it looked like the problem was solved. He did not want me to continue but to wait for the 'mechanic', I persisted and slipped the cover off. Then with some tissue paper the inside was dried out. The two points which open and close against a spring were cleaned by pulling a bit of rough cigarette packet cardboard through. Cover screwed back on. Bruooom, bruoom, it ran. From then on I started to become regarded as a mechanical wizard.

Likewise I was riding with friends when their car fan belt flew off (shown in most cars by a red 'not charging' light coming on and then usually the engine over-heats). Not belonging to any rescue organisation, and late at night in rural France there was no hope of getting a new belt till the next day. They were for calling a friend to come and pick us up when I said to tell them to bring some nylon tights or stockings. This took a lot of persuasion. But I'd used this old trick before, nylon tights are immensely strong and can do the job adequately which is simply to make the pulleys on the water pump and generator spin so there's not a great deal of resistance. By winding them around like a rope weaving their ends together so they won't fray you can get sufficient grip to turn both generator and water pump sufficiently enough to get you home. Which I did, it worked, we drove the car home, and the next day the right fan belt was bought and I slipped that on. Much to their amazement, I did not have a 'certificate' so how could I fix cars?

My reputation as a champion fixer consolidated further the time I arrived at Thierry's Paris flat after Vendange looking forward to a lazy drunken couple of days. These would be enlivened by watching his, at that time to a Brit, exotic and scarce, porn videos before going out to socialise.

France has always been more realistic and pragmatic about beautiful bodies and animal functions than us Protestant neighbours. Anyway my friend had accumulated a large collection of soft porn, nothing nasty and mostly quite well made movies. True they were mostly in French which was still difficult for me, but hey the narrative was not really an important feature. Anyway my arrival was with celebration (he loved Bernard's wine too) so we were sitting around digesting a late lunch and the second or third bottle when I asked for an old favourite to be put on. Suddenly he was not at all a happy

man. It seemed his VHS player had died the week before. This was early days and these were still expensive items so he had not yet bought a replacement. I asked if it was repairable, he said the shop had taken it, looked at it and had said not worth expense of trying to fix it. I asked if I could have a go. He didn't want me to; as I might damage it, I was not 'qualified, did not have an electrician's certificate'. His protests were ridiculous, I appealed to his Gallic logic, which evidently was no longer functioning any better than his video machine. I spelled it out.
"You said it does not work and the shop said it could not be repaired." I let that sink in by repeating it several times. "It's now a door-stop or fishing anchor, it has no value. What could I possibly now do to make it any worse or worth less? Go on let me try". Then reminding him of my previous miraculous repairs I won him over, okay nagged him into submission. I carefully unscrewed the panels and took the machine apart, over a newspaper in case any thing dropped out, which it did. A tiny metal cylinder I first mistook for a lighter flint. (In those days a metal 'flint' was rubbed on a thumb wheel creating a spark, and a micro-dust of potentially cancer initiating free radical oxides released over your fingers and face as you inhaled, whilst

lighting your probably marginally less toxic cigarette.)

I'd learned from years of experience trying to fix things that most faults are simple: fuses, switches, broken wires, broken contacts and just sometimes components burning out or falling off. Everything looked okay, fuses were checked with a torch battery and bulb, okay, nothing looked as if it had fried, there were no loose wires or bad connections I could spot (always worth checking the plug wiring, and also another power socket just in case). So I was left with had something 'fallen off' and there was that tiny 'flint'. I closely looked over all the moving parts, one of the mechanical linkages on the underside of the machine's deck, an actuating lever of some sort, one that moved as you pressed the start button, had a small apparently unused thus pointless hole, of a size, umm, YES, the 'flint' fitted into it. Another currently unused hole was discovered in another lever arm, this was manoeuvred in place and the flint now pushed through connecting both. Now we try pushing the button again, and yes one lever moved the other and everything now worked like clockwork. As I said, it's often simple, have a go, you may be surprised at your success.

My skills repairing things mechanical and electrical had started early on in my youth. I had enjoyed discovering how things worked and what they were made of, so early in my childhood I was taking things apart. Occasionally I learned how to put some of them back together.

This early interest became honed by running a series of very badly maintained motorcycles and cars experiencing an incredible number of roadside breakdowns. To be fair most of these vehicles had been in better fettle before I owned them, as I said they were badly maintained, so you learn on the job don't you…

Anyway one year for a change I foolishly chose to ride a motorcycle across France to the Vendange. After a series of more sporty machines I acquired a mundane BSA Bantam. This was a two-stroke (you put the oil in the petrol not the engine so it gives more power but smokes incessantly) pre-WW2 German design for their army, which after the war was built in the UK. Basic and probably reliable in its original German incarnation its main virtue was simplicity. With few tools and a hammer most jobs could be bodged. It could always be got going again, but only after much fiddling and at least one knuckle's worth of blood. Perhaps the greatest problem was the engine was a two-stroke so oil had to be accurately mixed with the petrol to lubricate it. Any error, and to be honest even just running it, meant the spark plug got oily. Which with weak electrics, worse when it was damp, meant annoyingly simple jobs such as removing and wiping clean the plug was needed rather too often. And also brackets and bits were continually vibrating with some eventually tending to fall off. Sometimes the vibration of the engine made your bones and teeth chatter, it could churn a bottle of milk into butter on the journey home.

It also had a vile trick, this as noted was a two stroke engine, as well as mixing the oil in with the petrol these have no valves in their cylinder head so were very simple devices. You kick started the engine and away you drove. Now if the ignition timing slipped, to which it was prone, it became harder and harder to start, and if it slipped one way suddenly it could start but bizarrely it could then be running in reverse. This was a known fault and thought unlikely to ever happen in practice, but of course it did. I'd just had the Bantam MOT'ed which was a safety examination by a licensed garage. Paying, folding the paper certificate in my pocket, I thanked them, sat on the bike, kicked the engine over, it started. I put it in gear and revving the engine slipped the clutch out expecting to set off forward as usual. Instead the damn thing lurched backwards in and under me clobbering me over in the muddy forecourt in the process, right in front of the garage mechanics. I stood up bedraggled and discomforted with pain, from bruised this and that and especially from my fuel tank caps embedding itself in my privates. No sympathy from the mechanics who were creased up with laughter. And incredulous in their surprise, for as I said everyone had thought this a rare occurrence unlikely to ever be witnessed, and they'd just seen a perfect example, they'd be dining out on that for years.

Therefore amongst the tasks to keep this engine running was to ensure the timing was spot on correct and to clean the points as these ignition parts are called. Simple enough, just pull a bit of dry cardboard between them. Likewise the same process was needed for the spark plug any time the engine began to splutter and it wasn't raining. To be able to keep going I sat spare spark plugs held upside down in the bottom of tubes of grit strapped to my front forks. I thought the bouncing and vibration would help clean them, which it did only fractionally, though at least this arrangement kept them dry. Unlike my riding gear which failed to keep me dry, assembled from many parts there were enough layers to make me resemble the Michelin Man logo. But this was the seventies, the materials were not 'modern', rain would seep through perhaps slowly but eventually. Still if enough layers even wet ones help keep you warm, or at least reduce the wind chill (simple tip, in emergency stuff a newspaper onto your chest next to your skin).

With a stack of multiple jackets, trousers and over-trousers, then boots and reflective bandoliers it took a while to put these all on followed by helmet, scarf and gloves. Although now weather proofed (well for at least an hour or so) this all made me feel heavy and stiff. No great problem bowling along the highway but not exactly ideal for push starting a recalcitrant Bantam in a thunderstorm, on the inner lane of a junction of a French motorway, about as bad a place you could find and where it had chosen to play up once again...

As mad as going back again every year to pick grapes had seemed to my friends this moved me to their ranking of more than half crazy. To choose to ride a motorbike through the low countries, across France to visit friends in Switzerland then on to the Vendange should have been cool, till they realised it was going to be on a BSA Bantam, I might as well have suggested a kids bicycle with trainer wheels. The idea seemed to them not just foolish but almost a joke, which was a tad unfair. Unexpectedly I got plenty of interest from locals whenever I stopped on my journey, which was more often than I wanted as reliability was a bit hit and miss, with more misses the wetter it got. It was because the Bantam looked its age, old, and thus was a tad interesting compared to the glitzy look of the modern bikes they were more used to seeing.

I did the classic and left without my passport and papers which I had taken out to check so often I then left them on the table. Having got halfway I had to call back to my friends to drive after me with these as I was too slow to return to get them. Fortunately they were able, caught me up and I took the ferry across the Merde du Nord from Felixstowe to Zeebrugge. This is a much longer voyage than the Dover crossing but in exchange saved the long ride down round London and on to Dover. I pop-pop-pop-popped through the Flanders region of Belgium then across northern France and over to Switzerland where I wanted to visit friends before going back across France down to the Vendange.

I knew getting the Bantam to drive up those Alpine roads would not be difficult just a lower gear and it would buzz up a steep slope fairly happily, but coming back down would be more of a challenge. With an old 2-stroke engine you have to keep allowing the engine to rev up every couple of minutes, because the oil is in the petrol so if too little petrol is consumed almost no oil is released. If you drive downhill continually using the engine for braking in gear on 'over-run' then too little or no oil at all reaches the internals and it soon seizes solid. But where thae road was quiet and all downhill I could sitch the engine off and just free wheel, a fantastic ride as near silent, though it was never legal to do so. Crossing the Continent I found French drivers unexpectedly gave more respect (room as they passed) to cyclists than I was used to, however motorcyclists were exempt. We were obviously fellow road competitors so treated accordingly as legitimate targets and a challenge to every other driver's manhood. Just the sight of me pootling along would force their cars to be driven even more frenetically until they could get past and leave me in the dust. Which as the Bantam was not exactly very speedy and I was in no hurry was not difficult. But even elderly vehicles long overdue for the breaker's yard would have to somehow be made to get past me. I've no problem with this as such. However riding a motorbike on an empty road is relatively safe, riding with some wine addled driver in a flying piece of shrapnel anywhere near, behind, passing or in front, is not comfortable. Worse if they are so underpowered they cannot pull away then they expose you to their foolishness for far too long. Likewise trucks would leave too little space when passing, especially on the faster main roads when their slipstream could bowl you over -if they did not side swipe you first.

Thus I loved small roads with little traffic, ones where if anyone wanted to get past I could simply pull over to let them by. I had drawn a nearly straight line across the map to follow avoiding the busiest bigger roads taking slower scenic routes. I was proficient at map reading so found this little difficulty, especially as French roads were amazingly well signed. It was all so easy if you simply planned to ride from village to village, even if meandering, but I loved that.

As the evening approached I simply pulled over in a small town and asked some folk where a modestly priced hotel was, one was pointed out to me. They were also of course a restaurant and only to pleased to have an extra customer. And kindly helped me lock 'my valuable steed' in their garage, apparently if left outside it might disappear. (I was happy for the extra security though doubted anyone would be able to start it I guessed it might still be pushed away, or bits removed as souvenirs.)

With a splendid meal and wine inside me life seemed good. The bed was comfortable and I slept till wakened at dawn by a nearby cockerel.

No problem, pleased to be up, and after coffee and a croissant back on the road. It was fine autumn weather and the miles, well kilometres, pop, pop, popped by. I arrived at my friends in Switzerland just as dusk was falling. An excellent ride, mainly as it had been dry, and stunningly beautiful scenery almost the whole way. After a couple of days enjoying the (lower) Alps I needed to get to Beaujolais for the start of the Vendange. This was also taken along another nearly straight line through a multitude of villages, though the countryside was more up and down than I'd expected. And slower going, this was taking longer than anticipated, and I'd set off extra early allowing for breakdowns. Which with dry weather were only every so often, more as a reminder than serious issues. Night was approaching, a Bantam is not a very fast motorbike, and the headlight was dire, barely a glimmer, I wondered whether it was designed like this to prevent aircraft spotting you and had not been upgraded for civilian use. Effectively you had to have the night vision of a cat or be very brave to drive at night and I was now doing so. Thank goodness I had already been there picking over several years so as I got closer I knew the general directions to take, though it seemed interminable, and all the way up hill. As I started to recognise places I knew the roads better and better. Though still flying near blind in the dark I was desperate to get there, and finally arrived at Bernard's farm. I gratefully pop-popped down his drive to the astounded, some hostile, looks of several folk assembled in the yard. Of course they did not know it was me under all the gear, Bernard knew I was coming by bike but they had no idea. I popped, putt, putted to as top, took my helmet off, those who knew me from previous years could barely believe it was me. *FROM ENGLAND!* On that old motorbike! When I told them I'd sojourned in Switzerland on the way they were even more disbelieving. But they were won over after I took them in turns for spins round the local roads, eventually making a trip all the way up Mont Brouilly just to prove it would do it. However for the duration of the Vendange I left the Bantam stood in a barn and gave the key to Bernard to safeguard. There was no way I was going to risk riding it around when drunk, what and ruin my means of getting home carrying more bottles than I could carry unaided. And there was no way I was going to remain sober. That year once the Vendange was over I wanted to get to my friends in Paris rapidly as some parties were planned, thus I had to take the larger busier roads. Still once popping along a Bantam will often keep going (well in the dry) and the distance is covered, just not as fast as by everyone else squeezing screamingly close as they pass you by.

Then came the most fearsome highway of all, one I would have to dice with, cannot be avoided. I do not think it is my prejudice, I'm sure even the French would admit it is insane traffic on The 'Perri-frique' (should be Very-Freak) a motorway ring-road running around Paris. Here the rules of the road seemed to have gone missing, even more than on other roads. The rules on the French road are in general similar as those of most civilised countries, though often more ignored, except on the Perri-frique. Here they were not often ignored but always as if compulsory or a challenge. It seemed every driver no matter what vehicle was competing for their life's honour, first come first… Frightening, all the time, all the way.

Now I had ridden powerful motorcycles and to be fair the Bantam was just not fast enough for the road conditions which would have been much less frightening on a bike with more serious ability. Pottering along flat out, at the most 50mph/80kph, in the nearside lane seemed I was given no more respect nor distance than a large piece of road-kill. Even so it was the nimbleness of my motorbike that saved me when I had an incredibly lucky escape from a serious pile-up where a second sooner or later either way could have been fatal. In a tunnelled section a car hurtled down a slip road not slowing and driving full pelt right into three lanes of speeding traffic as if no vehicles were there, hitting several vehicles these hitting others causing a huge pile up.

I saw it all coming, then happening, as did many car drivers, but we were all moving at speed too close together in every lane and they had nowhere to go. But I being small and on the inside lane managed to somehow get through gaps veering and swerving past crashing cars in the melee coming out untouched while in my mirrors all was mayhem. I kept going too scared to slow down, barely believing I had made it through what had looked seriously terminal. As I kept riding it became obvious the accident had blocked the road entirely as I was now on my own on an empty multi-lane highway, not a car or truck coming from behind me. While on the opposite side streams of flashing lights and sirens were heading the other direction. I could be no help, and little value as yet another witness, so I rode on thanking my lucky stars and now enjoying having the whole multilane highway to myself with no more trucks whizzing too close by me.

However in the congested stop start traffic of Paris the Bantam proved more suited, and only one among many even more pedestrian machines buzzing around. On the open road I'd felt a target, here I was still a target but now in a shoal and thus 'safer'. I pop pop popped along the streets feeling relieved as they became more familiar and when I reached my friends they were more than a little impressed that I arrived at all. I'd successfully made a tour of France they'd have found hard going in a car.

Of course they knew I'd just been to the Vendange at Bernard's and that I'd have a lot of bottles of The Best but they were surprised when I showed I'd brought three dozen bottles on my bike. Along with the twenty in my rucksack there were another half dozen each side in panniers and more in a bag on a rack behind the seat which also held the two stroke oil and spares. They decided it was their duty to make my return safer by lightening my load. I duly obliged and we had some excellent wining with our dining over the next few days, though I carefully retained most of my hard won bottles to get me through the long year waiting before I could come back to get any more.

After my recovery in Paris I left in miserable weather and with several unplanned stops to dry out the engine I finally made it to the ferry okay. But on berthing in England when I tried to start the Bantam to drive off the ferry naturally it would not fire, push starting it was impossible as the exit ramp and road was uphill. I slowly, so slowly, pushed my heavily loaded Bantam up and into the Customs House where I was the last arrival. Indeed all others had gone as I pushed on up to a table and a smirking Customs Officer. He seemed amused by my efforts, anyway he asked if I had anything to declare, and I said I had no fags or spirits just a couple of crates of wine. He laughed at my 'joke' and waved me on. With several failed efforts to his further amusement, I eventually managed to bump start the bike on the flat way out then pop-pop-popped my way home, with my two dozen bottles!

You see each year Bernard gave every picker on leaving their traditional two bottles, and bonus bottles for those he most appreciated. Moreover most years some pickers would be Muslim and only too happy to give up their bottles for no more than a token or even a handshake. Thus each year I managed to bring home more and more. I had an ex-military ruck-sack with massive capacity. I carefully wrapped each bottle in newspaper then inserted it in a sock. Pairs of these were wrapped in t-shirts to be carefully layered alternately in the main compartment where I could fit a dozen and a half padded about with more clothes. A couple more would fit in the side pockets. My few other belongings, mostly books, were strapped in pouches buckled on top. This was all very heavy, and worse unwieldy.

I learnt to sit the rucksack on the ground, shuffle back into it then come up into a squat, and with the aid of one hand holding onto something solid I could make the lift. Once vertical with the load comfortably set I had to watch my step as I was now so top heavy, especially difficult was going down stairs. At the border it was the same procedure as on the Bantam, I'd walk up to the Customs and answer no cigs, no spirits, and twenty bottles of wine. They'd look amused and wave me on. Only once in a dozen years was I ever examined when they were so impressed by the actual load of twenty bottles I really was carrying they excused the duty, after all I'd given a completely honest declaration!

One journey back, on a train coming into my next station, I was getting ready to squat and lift when a kind passenger suddenly tried to assist without asking me. He obviously saw my pack was heavy and had just wanted to help. However he simply did not realise quite how heavy this was and I'd not have been surprised if he pulled his back as he lifted it up for me by inexpertly bending over. With a really heavy load you use your legs keeping the mass close in and low to your body, bending over to lift something is how to hurt yourself.

Although I usually hitched I sometimes trained, and once took a very very slow train, by accident of my poor French rather than intent. I had given up hitching as the weather had turned torrential almost as soon as I'd got into France. Nobody wants to pick up a dripping wet passenger so soaked through I walked to, I think it was Amiens train station, asked for an inexpensive ticket down to Macon, was so pleased I had managed to do this and find the right platform and train and started my unexpected trip. I had managed to get the stations where I changed written down but not the times, and not realised this ticket was inexpensive for most of my trains were not 'express' so stopped at every, often quaint, station you could wish for.

As even a slow train is faster than hitching, and in the wet much more convenient I actually enjoyed that long journey but immediately preferred the amazing ride on the new TGV when that first arrived.

Train of great speed, this ran from Paris to the South on brand new rails, now also from London through the tunnel.) It was like getting on an airplane, sleek, smooth and unbelievably fast. A distance that had taken a whole days travel before flashed past in a couple of hours. It was so far ahead of our British Rail / Snail of the time. However it was also like a plane in that you had to book your seat.

Once the TGV was available I loved this, I could arrive at Macon station a short drive or hitch from Bernard's only hours after leaving Paris. Of course this seemed to be quite a busy station with huge numbers of folk arriving then leaving the Vendange all at the same time as myself. One year though I had stayed on at the farm for a while to cycle round the region borrowing Bernard's bike. As part of one last trip I'd be riding almost past the station so planned to drop in to book my seat for the following day. Rode up to find the station unexpectedly quiet and almost empty. Of course the crush I'd expected was only witnessed for those few weeks of Vendange which was now well over. For the rest of the year this was a small quiet station. The guys on duty saw me cycling up and let me know if I was taking the bicycle it would need booking in along with reserving my seat. Despite my awkward Franglais they then happily chatted away for some time about the joy of cycling around the region, turned out both were competitive club cyclists. Then naturally the Vendange and the vintage were all discussed, they had time to fill.

Eventually one decided it was getting close to lunch so we got round to actually booking my ticket. I showed my paperwork and was finally asked which train, and where I wanted to sit. Having answered the first question as Paris where I'm off to 'for the wine, women and song' as I quipped, I then answered the second question with and "I'd love my seat to be next to a beautiful lady". They smiled, it was France, gave me my reservation receipt and with a hearty waving off from them I cycled away for the rest of my day's journey around the region. Early the following morning Bernard drove me over and dropped me at the station, I waited in the mist on the platform. The sleek missile hissed alongside and halted, I found my carriage, it was near empty as I counted down to my seat. Which was next to one of the three occupied seats in the whole compartment, and sitting there was a beautiful young lady… Somehow, and I can't work out how, they had complied with my jocular request, such could only happen in France…

By the time, still a few hours even at such speed, we arrived at Paris we were getting on nicely, she had been fascinated by my tales of Vendange, particularly my references to the quality of the wine and how I had a cache.and now she was taking me to her favourite places in

Paris. Which tour I enjoyed immensely, though mind you she got me treating us to high tea at a classy café in the Rue de Rivoli. A beautiful place from between the wars this took most of my hard won cash as it was eye wateringly expensive, wonderful and exquisite experience though. I stayed with her only a short while and left when she started looking a serious threat to my haul of wine. It had been a mistake to share a bottle with her, more-so the second. Anyway for she was not just French she was dedicated to drinking fine wine, and she had immediately twigged just how good mine was. I'd planned to eke out most of my bottles over the whole of the coming year. I could see them disappearing in a delightful drunken frenzy in but a few days. I took my sack of treasure and quietly snuck off to my friends.

As futuristic as the TGV most certainly was it was rivalled by most of the Metro in Paris. Whereas travelling on much of London Underground could have been fairly described as a "Victorian Experience', and the Northern Line as 'Dickensian' over in Paris it was CLEAN. Larger glassier trains than our rattlers whooshed into the stations on rubber wheels. How sensible rather than the squealing squeaking metal on metal of our tube.

Things reverted when you arrived at the Gare du Nord station for the North and Great Britain where, eventually, you could board the Night Ferry train. The least expensive travel option this had 'good old' British rolling stock, no modern TGV or Metro glitz here, some of it still carried more than a whiff of coal smoke. Corridor trains, these had a narrow passageway passing alongside individual compartments which each squeezed in eight or so passengers in two pairs of four facing each other behind a sliding door. People would go to all sorts of efforts to try and occupy a whole compartment or at least half of one as then they might be able to snatch some sleep laying *along* one of the two bench seats. Folk tried claiming seats were 'taken' with a coat or hat, or 'reserved', or pulling down the blinds on the sliding doors. As the train was always over-crowded all these ploys were ineffective, but still tried.

One neat if weird method I discovered that could work was to be exuberantly inviting. As each prospect slid open the door I would blurt out.
" Oh please come in, have a seat, look that one is free. Oh do come in, I'm so pleased to meet you."
If they obey or rather ignore me and keep coming in I'd continue
 "Have you heard the word of the lord, do you know god is talking to you, you only have to

listen. Open up your heart, the way of sin leads to eternal damnation."

If even this spiel failed to deter then I delivered my masterpiece

"I'm so happy, my voices said they'd be sending someone for me to save, there's so much I need to help you with…"

This often worked like magic, well with almost every native English passenger who'd promptly reverse out preferring to sit on the toilet floor than endure my obviously lunatic socially inappropriate company. The ploy did not work so well with other nationalities whether they spoke English really well or not at all. They mostly just assumed, rightly in a way, that I was another of those English eccentrics they came across, mad, maddening, but not usually actually dangerous except by accident.

Of course keeping a compartment to yourself assumes you had managed to actually get on the Night Ferry Train at all. This had an erratic nature and was oft delayed, this meant waiting in the Gare du Nord station, sometimes till late into the night or worse into the next day. This was not a place seemingly designed for waiting with barely any comfort for delayed passengers. At night everything closed, then the Gendarmes would come round checking everyone's papers, and as long as you had a ticket they were curt but reasonably civil. But woe betide you if you were delayed till when the night cleaners arrived, they were far brusquer, downright brutal and soon had you moved out of their way. As dire as was the Night Ferry train the Night Ferry itself was worse, this had yet older more dilapidated conditions. The trains were at least randomly heated, a luxury not yet available to stowage passengers on a cross channel cattle barge it seemed. There always seemed seriously insufficient numbers of seats for the number of passengers, god help us if there enough spaces in the lifeboats should we need them. The boat toilets were far more unpleasant than the most neglected either English or French trains possessed, which were themselves quite disgusting. Old age and a lack of scrupulous cleansing meant they had a bad start but on this disgusting layer was embellished the dreaded Mal de mer. This was an added bonus on many if not most Channel crossings, for the Night Ferry sailed regardless of all but hurricanes.

The boat would be hurled about and almost every passenger scared shitless as well as stomach-less. One time I saw the boat yank itself down and away from a man descending a stairway. He idiotically had not grasped the handrail and so was suddenly left suspended up in the air, then even worse as he fell the boat returned and came back up under him with a whack breaking bones. I often avoided the melee inside and felt better, and the air was sweeter, when I dared to sit outside. Though this could be even scarier as the horizon jerked all over the place and you felt you might be thrown off.

One year I decided it was worth trying the new hovercraft crossing, not to save time but just to avoid the night time horror show. It was okay but not pleasant, indeed the speed was most advantageous as the discomfort of the journey was over relatively quickly. But it was noisy, bumpy, smelly, bumpy, noisy, bumpy and scary. I was almost relieved when my return was cancelled because of bad weather, only to find I was transferred onto the Night Ferry which was sailing regardless.

Most years on my way home I would spend some time in Paris with friends I made at college and mostly with Thierry a relative of Bernard who I had met when he picked grapes with us one year. A student he had rented a tiny top flat in an ancient building, a classic French apartment block with concierge guarding downstairs and tall winding stairways all the way up into the roof. Thierry's kitchenette had a sloping ceiling with a small glass roof-light that could be opened. You could stick your head out and you were gazing over the roof and beyond to the whole city, an incredible view.

Over several years Thierry expanded the flat, he had noticed how there was one more window on the front of the block than rooms, and investigating found a hidden space. This had been boxed off in some long forgotten conversion, presumably because it had a rather low sloping ceiling impinging on most of it, but that was fine for an extra bedroom. Then he reckoned if they had boxed off that piece maybe there were more along that side, and found another, this windowless, but still usable space. His tiny flat had become a warren, and a perfect place for student friends to come and stay. Especially as this was in the heart of old Paris with streets full of family shops all round. Oh the smells, the cheeses, the fresh baguettes.

Many of his friends were students at Nanterre University, a hot bed of activism at the time with whole blocks burnt down. One day they all came back very excited after a big demonstration. I was a bit taken aback as they unloaded baseball bats and cobble stones from the boot of their car. Seemed they'd not been needed anyway. They'd gone to be the left wing counter demonstration to a larger right wing one. They were really enervated, I slowly grasped the picture. It seemed the riot police had beat up the right wing demonstration relieving my friends of any need to get involved. And this was what was pleasing them even more, they had previously thought the police were biased and would beat them up because being students they were left wing. That may have been so, but they were chuffed because they'd seen that many riot police obviously just enjoyed beating anyone up regardless of persuasion.

One year I went to Lyon and St Etienne before visiting Paris. I had made friends over the years with some pickers who wanted to show me round their home towns. Now although they were of Algerian descent and theoretically Muslim some were lax followers and enjoyed alcohol. Though mostly as beer or spirits for they considered they were only forbidden wine, which had been pretty hard on them picking grapes. Now I was used to drinking heavily but I was in for an education with these guys. 'Pastis' is slightly reduced from the military grade rocket fuel known as Absinthe. You may have come across Pernod the most popular commercial brand, Ricard is less known though preferred in much of France, and there are many local varieties of pastis, some contraband, most ought to be. All are very strong, aniseed flavoured spirits somewhat like Vermouth, they turn cloudy when mixed with iced water. And all are fearsome ways to get drunk, with an appalling hangover to follow. That first morning in Lyon I was drinking one to every two that each of my compatriots were knocking back. By lunch or should I say lurch I was legless, as were my friends. First and only time I've witnessed someone walk full on face into a street lamp post. Owww.

Lyon was a great city, far less expensive than Paris and with some excellent local delicacies such as quenelle I mentioned earlier. One favourite everywhere was a dessert cake, a choux pastry confection called Religieuse or Nun from the shape and decoration. One small hollow choux pastry ball atop one large hollow sphere of choux pastry, both filled with vanilla, chocolate or coffee sweet cream, sat on an almond macaroon biscuit, coated with a coffee or chocolate glaze then embellished with piped icing cream to look like wee nuns. Delicious death by calories. Those around Lyons were especially good, though later when told this was taken as a challenge by my Chauvinistic Parisian friends who then dragged me to a half dozen patisseries to see if we could not find a better. What a lovely challenge if tooth and waistline destroying, and although I love sickly sweet stuff towards the end I must admit I was losing my will to go on.

Not as much as I lost enthusiasm later with my friend Thierry's father who was a gourmet of French charcuterie especially saucissons, sausages. As I said I generally did not eat much meat but was always curious and interested in a taste of anything new. Well he came well provided with a vast selection and gave us a thin slice of this and that with a long explanation of their contents and pedigree. I must admit many were tasty, though one was much like black pudding and I did not much like its heavy blood flavour. But worst to me, was, and I remember the name to this day, Andouillet, which seemed indistinguishable to an oily condom tightly packed with finely sliced, garlic flavoured, oily condoms. I really could not get any enthusiasm for that delicacy, but 'chacun sont gout', each to their own taste.

If you ask me what do I remember most fondly from my time grape picking in France it has to be The Wine, though The Food comes close, as does The Backache. Sadly after returning over a dozen years I slowly became less enamoured. First with the passing of the years I discovered I could no longer drink red wine ad lib so was finding it harder to wake up, get up and work as I once had originally. Bernard did not want to lose me of course, indeed my last season he presented me with a 'tasse vin' (special tasting cup) in honour of my dozen years. But he knew as did I that it was a young man's game and I was getting older, and with more commitments back in the UK it became harder to find the time.

I never told him though one reason I stopped was the food. First, forced by modern logic he tried to save time and cost by cutting out the second breakfast. This aggrieved me, especially as I'd lobbied for a short 'tea-break' in the afternoon as well, having noted how we worked harder with renewed enthusiasm after a break. The lack of second breakfast seemed a cruel loss and was disrupting such a long tradition. And was hard for me as I seldom want to eat much soon after arising but prefer a later meal, which the second breakfast in the fields filled perfectly. But far worse, disastrously so, grandmother even with assistance could no longer manage to produce so many meals in short succession. Plus economic pressure meant the wonderful home grown and local food became replaced with more of the commercially produced and less and less of the wonderfully home made. I understand the reasons and do not criticise this as such, but the change took away so much of my reason for being there.

Ironically it was the I Ching that had heralded my arrival and then signalled time for that final decision for me. I said I consulted it regularly. Well that day when I was pondering whether to say I'd be back again the next season I asked and it said Wei Chei, after completion, I should desist, go forward and not look back. It was correct for I had had the offer of teaching Evening Classes which started during the same period, and my garden had become a smallholding with animals and plants under cover to look after. It was finally time to move on, to say Fin to Vin and Vendange.

Three nearly four decades later I still miss it all, my friends, the countryside, the atmosphere, the vines, the wine, the food, the life at the table, the camaraderie. Sadly because of the foolishness of Brexit my children cannot have their turn, and I am now loathe to even go visit for the poignancy this may cause, for surely so many will have passed away during the many intervening years. Yet every year my thoughts turn eastwards each autumn as the many vines I've planted in my garden here ripen and colour and I feel deeply, profoundly, nostalgic.

The Vendange was a great adventure, and although a brash young chap when I started I'm so grateful for over those dozen years I matured into a more serious man, a writer and a gardener with an especial enduring love and profound respect for vines, wines and grapes, for as I punned earlier, it was the Vendange gave me my Raisin d'être.

Fin

Bob's other books, self published

What to do When
Timely notes of monthly tasks in each and every area of the garden, "there's a right time for every job- and it was probably last month", very handy for newer gardeners who are taking it all on the first time, and also for us older hands who are not keeping up as well as we did

Really help your plants
Plants and other plants, their good & bad companions and worst weeds' Volume I of 'Plant Companions and Co-lives'
An A-Z of wild and garden plants and recorded effects between these and other plants we need to know about whenever planning or planting our gardens.

Really Help Butterflies
Being Volume II of 'Plant Companions and Co-lives'
There's little point planting 'flowers to help butterflies' any more than making the North sea bigger to help cod stocks. We need <u>grow those plants their larvae eat</u>. This is an A-Z of wild and garden plants and which of our native butterfly caterpillars THEIR FOLIAGE will sustain.

Really help your garden ecology
Plants and co-lives; their associated fauna: insects, nematodes, bacteria, fungi large & small and shared viruses
this being Volume III of 'Plant Companions and Co-lives'
Interactions between our native and garden plants and all the varied forms of life they coexist with and not covered in volumes I & II.

Really help your crops
An edited compilation of all three above volumes for the most important interactions, those with our crop plants.
An indispensable aid to more effective cultivation.

Pulpit in the potting shed
My 'philosophy' expressed in limerick, verse and songs written over five decades.
Fifty essays in rhyme, terse verse & dirty ditties.
A pen-chant to word play.

Grow Your Own Kitchen garden & Pantry
This is invaluable, not just how to grow but all the ways to then store, preserve & process your crops, an essential guide to becoming your own delicatessen.

Greenhouse, cloche and tunnel gardening, Growing under cover
40 years of experience of protected cropping distilled into this volume including historical development, ways and means, what you need to consider, what you can grow with practical advice on each.

Recycle & Reuse stuff in your garden
My first e-book and best seller, not ever been printed to save paper, exactly what the cover says; simple garden upcycling uses for all sorts of waste products and junk.
You may use, repeat, copy, distribute by any means any idea from this book with my blessing.

a foreign county -my AutobyBobraphy
Book one, early years, 1953-65
rural life in the fifties, remnants of an old world now gone, from farming with horses to the space age in one leap, and a school more Gormenghast & Whacko than Hogwarts

Bob's books with other publishers, mostly now out of print though widely available pre-loved.

The Companion Garden (Good Companions in USA) (pub. Kyle Cathie)
My first published book was a delightful little illustrated volume of the benefits mixing plants can offer to us, other creatures and each other. (Several editions all sadly out of print with signed copies of first hardback now quite collectable.)

Bob Flowerdew's Complete Book of Companion Gardening (Kyle Cathie)
I explore the numerous ways plants interact with other flora and fauna about them, with historical observations, and how we can use these to our advantage.
I find it hard to understand why some alleged 'scientists' claim companion planting is baseless. It would be stranger still if with hundreds of thousands of plants and critters in our gardens to find that none interacted in any way other than by being eaten.

The Organic Gardener (Hamlyn-Reed Octopus)
Organic methods in detail including an illustrated plan view of my garden, full of

luscious photos of my flowers and produce taken by Jerry Harpur.
In soft back as Bob Flowerdew's Organic Garden. Now sadly out of print though re-worked and re-issued in updated revised forms as **Go Organic**, and **Organic Garden Basics** (Hamlyns).

Bob Flowerdew's Complete Fruit Book (Kyle Cathie)
An encyclopaedic testimonial to the delights fruits and nuts offer to the gardener, the gourmet and to us all.
Full descriptions, instructions and alternative uses, and with my own recipes. Includes not just the usual soft and orchard fruits but also those we can glean from the wild, those unknown edible ornamentals, and those fruits you may come across in a good supermarket or on a foreign holiday. Now out in a carefully revised and expanded edition, and in nearly two dozen foreign languages.
Also combined with Jekka's Complete Herb, and Matthew Bigg's Complete Vegetables in a comprehensive edible encyclopaedia of Vegetables, herbs and fruit (Kyle Cathie).

Bob Flowerdew's Organic Bible (Kyle Cathie)
How to be Organic.
Very beautiful photographs (204) in this book all taken in my garden are in themselves lasting testimonials to the methods, and to the exquisite quality of Organic flowers, fruits and vegetables. All you really need to know.

The No work garden (Kyle Cathie)
In this comic diatribe of vitriol poured enthusiastically on the heads of experts, designers and instant garden makeovers I explain how much of conventional gardening advice is not wrong but is rather inappropriate. I show easier ways of getting more pleasure & production from your garden for much less effort or expense. Good for non-expert gardeners, and older hands will also find much to amuse and inform.

The Gourmet Gardener (Kyle Cathie) -
With the emphasis on quality; it's all about taste, flavour, texture, variety and seasonality. This book is not about feeding a family of twelve from an allotment, or just how to produce fodder reliably. It is all about producing really tasty tucker. Growing the very best for yourself!

Going Organic (Kyle Cathie)
The greener gardeners guide to solving pest, disease & cultural problems a gardener will likely encounter, along with their most natural cures and preventatives.
 A comprehensive introduction to all the greener organic methods you can employ to avoid pitfalls & errors, woes & foes and also as a reference book for the commoner pests, diseases and their solutions.

Grow your own, Eat your own (Kyle Cathie)
My idiosyncratic but very pragmatic approach, this time to storing and preserving your own produce. It is not difficult to grow lots of your own delicious produce but far harder to do so over the whole year.
Growing food is only half the story, you also need to harvest, store, process and preserve in a host of different ways to feed your family more fully and happily- so be your own delicatessen, confectioner and brewer as well as greengrocer and cook.
Also published in French!

Bob's Basics (Kyle Cathie)
Six compact volumes covering the most important areas of greener and organic gardening, their titles say it all.
Composting
Companion Planting
Weeding without chemicals
Pruning, Training and Tidying
Simple green Pest and Disease control
Sowing, Planting, Watering and Feeding

Bob also co-authored-

The complete book of vegetables, herbs and fruit - available in many languages and editions
The complete manual of Organic Gardening
Gardeners Question Time All Your Problems Solved
Gardeners Question Time Plant Chooser
Gardeners Question Time Tips & Techniques

Plus there is much useful information gratis on my website www.bobflowerdew.com and daily notes on what's happening in my garden on X/Twitter @FlowerdewBob

Printed in Great Britain
by Amazon